Exit the King

one of us

Other Works by Eugene Ionesco
Published by Grove Press

EXIT THE KING

by

Eugène Ionesco

Translated from the French
by Donald Watson

Grove Press, Inc.
New York

Exit The King was first performed on December 15, 1962 at the Théâtre de l'Alliance Française in Paris. An English version was later performed at the Edinburgh Festival in September, 1963 by the Royal Court Company.

The American première was performed by APA Repertory Company by arrangement with the APA Phoenix on September 1, 1967 in Los Angeles. It was directed by Ellis Rabb, with music by Conrad Susa, scenery design by Rouben Ter-Arutunian, lighting design by James Tilton, costumes design by Nancy Potts, and with the following cast:

BERENGER THE FIRST, *The King*	Richard Easton
QUEEN MARGUERITE, *First Wife*	Louise Latham
QUEEN MARIE, *Second Wife*	Patricia Conolly
THE DOCTOR, *who is also Surgeon, Executioner,* *Bacteriologist & Astrologist*	Will Geer
JULIETTE, *Domestic Help and* *Registered Nurse*	Pamela Payton-Wright
THE GUARD	Nicolas Martin

The photographs used throughout the text are from the APA Repertory Company production and were taken by Van Williams.

The Set

The throne room, vaguely dilapidated, vaguely Gothic. In the center of the stage, against the back wall, a few steps leading to the King's throne. On either side, downstage, two smaller thrones—those of the two QUEENS, *his wives.*

Upstage left, a small door leading to the King's apartments. Upstage right, another small door. Also on the right, downstage, a large door. Between these two doors, a Gothic window. Another small window on the left of the stage; and another small door downstage, also on the left. Near the large door, an old GUARD *with a halberd.*

Before and during the rise of the curtain, and for a few minutes afterward, you can hear a derisive rendering of regal music reminiscent of the King's Levee in the seventeenth century.

*Ionesco's own suggested cuts
are indicated in the text
by square brackets.*

GUARD (*announcing*): His Majesty the King, Berenger the First. Long live the King!

The KING *enters from the little door on the right, wearing a deep crimson cloak, with a crown on his head and a scepter in his hand, rapidly crosses the stage and goes off through the upstage door on the left.*

(*Announcing:*) Her Majesty Queen Marguerite, First Wife to the King, followed by Juliette, Domestic Help and Registered Nurse to their Majesties. Long live the Queen!

MARGUERITE, *followed by* JULIETTE, *enters through the downstage door on the left and goes out through the large door.*

(*Announcing:*) Her Majesty Queen Marie, Second Wife to the King, but first in affection, followed by Juliette, Domestic Help and Registered Nurse to their Majesties. Long live the Queen!

MARIE, *followed by* JULIETTE, *enters through the large door on the right and goes out with* JULIETTE *through the downstage door on the left.* MARIE *appears younger and more beautiful than* MARGUERITE. *She has a crown and a deep crimson cloak. She is wearing jewels. Her cloak is of more modern style and looks as if it comes from a high-class couturier. The* DOCTOR *comes in through the upstage door on the right.*

(*Announcing:*) His Notability, Doctor to the King,

7

Gentleman Court Surgeon, Bacteriologist, Executioner and Astrologist.

The DOCTOR *comes to the center of the stage and then, as though he had forgotten something, turns back the way he came and goes out through the same door. The* GUARD *remains silent for a few moments. He looks tired. He rests his halberd against the wall, and then blows into his hands to warm them.*

I don't know, this is just the time when it ought to be hot. Central heating, start up! Nothing doing, it's not working. Central heating, start up! The radiator's stone cold. It's not my fault. He never told me he'd taken away my job as Chief Firelighter. Not officially, anyway. You never know with them.

Suddenly, he picks up his weapon. QUEEN MARGUERITE *reappears through the upstage door on the right. She has a crown on her head and is wearing a deep crimson cloak that is a bit shabby. She looks rather severe. She stops in the center, downstage. She is followed by* JULIETTE.

Long live the Queen!

MARGUERITE (*to* JULIETTE, *looking around her*): There's a lot of dust about. And cigarette butts on the floor.

JULIETTE: I've just come from the stables milking the cow, your Majesty. She's almost out of milk. I haven't had time to do the living room.

MARGUERITE: This is *not* the living room. It's the throne room. How often do I have to tell you?

JULIETTE: All right, the throne room, as your Majesty wishes. I haven't had time to do the living room.

MARGUERITE: It's cold.

GUARD: I've been trying to turn the heat on, your Majesty. Can't get the system to function. The radiators won't co-operate. The sky is overcast and the clouds don't seem to want to break up. The sun's late. And yet I heard the King order him to come out.

MARGUERITE: Is that so! The sun's already deaf to his commands.

GUARD: I heard a little rumble during the night. There's a crack in the wall.

MARGUERITE: Already? Things are moving fast. I wasn't expecting this so soon.

GUARD: Juliette and I tried to patch it up.

JULIETTE: He woke me in the middle of the night, when I was sound asleep!

GUARD: And now it's here again. Shall we have another try?

MARGUERITE: It's not worth it. We can't turn the clock back. (*To* JULIETTE:) Where's Queen Marie?

JULIETTE: She must still be dressing.

MARGUERITE: Naturally!

JULIETTE: She was awake before dawn.

MARGUERITE: Oh! Well, that's something!

JULIETTE: I heard her crying in her room.

MARGUERITE: Laugh or cry, that's all she can do. (*To* JULIETTE:) Let her be sent for at once. Go and fetch her.

Just at this minute, QUEEN MARIE *appears, dressed as described above.*

GUARD (*a moment before Queen Marie's entrance*): Long live the Queen!

MARGUERITE (*to* MARIE): Your eyes are quite red, my dear. It spoils your beauty.

MARIE: I know.

MARGUERITE: Don't start crying again!

MARIE: I can't really help it.

MARGUERITE: Don't go to pieces, whatever you do. What's the use? It's the normal course of events, isn't it? You were expecting it. Or had you stopped expecting it?

MARIE: *You've* been *waiting* for it!

MARGUERITE: A good thing, too. And now the moment's arrived. (*To* JULIETTE:) Well, why don't you give her another handkerchief?

MARIE: I was still hoping . . .

MARGUERITE: You're wasting your time. Hope! (*She shrugs her shoulders.*) Nothing but hope on their lips and tears in their eyes. What a way to behave!

MARIE: Have you seen the Doctor again? What did he say?

MARGUERITE: What you've heard already.

MARIE: Perhaps he's made a mistake.

MARGUERITE: Don't start hoping all over again! The signs are unmistakable.

MARIE: Perhaps he's misinterpreted them.

MARGUERITE: There's no mistaking the signs, if you look at them objectively. And you know it!

MARIE (*looking at the wall*): Oh! That crack!

MARGUERITE: Oh! You've seen it, have you? And that's not the only thing. It's your fault if he's not prepared. It's your fault if it takes him by surprise. You let him go his own way. You've even led him astray. Oh yes! Life was very sweet. With your fun and games, your dances, your processions, your official dinners, your winning ways and your fireworks displays, your silver spoons and your honeymoons! How many honeymoons have you had?

MARIE: They were to celebrate our wedding anniversaries.

MARGUERITE: You celebrated them four times a year. "We've got to *live*" you used to say. . . . But one must never forget.

MARIE: He's so fond of parties.

MARGUERITE: People know and carry on as if they didn't. They know and they forget. But *he* is the King. *He* must not forget. He should have his eyes fixed in front of him, know every stage in the journey, know exactly how long the road, and never lose sight of his destination.

MARIE: My poor darling, my poor little King.

MARGUERITE (*to* JULIETTE): Give her another handkerchief. (*To* MARIE:) Be a little more cheerful, can't you? Tears are catching. He's weak enough already. What a pernicious influence you've had on him. But there! I'm afraid he liked you better than me! I wasn't at all jealous, I just realized he wasn't being very wise. And now you can't help him any more. Look at you! Bathed in tears. You're not defying me now. You've lost that challenging look. Where's it all gone, that brazen insolence, that sarcastic smile? Come on now, wake up! Take your proper place and try to straighten up. Think! You're still wearing your beautiful necklace! Come along! Take your place!

MARIE (*seated*): I'll never be able to tell him.

MARGUERITE: I'll see to that. I'm used to the chores.

MARIE: And don't *you* tell him either. No, no, please. Don't say a word, I beg you.

MARGUERITE: *Please* leave it to me. We'll still want you, you know, later, still need you during the ceremony. You like official functions.

MARIE: Not this one.

MARGUERITE (*to* JULIETTE): You. Spread our trains out properly.

JULIETTE: Yes, your Majesty. (JULIETTE *does so.*)

MARGUERITE: I agree it's not so amusing as all your charity balls. Those dances you get up for children, and old folks, and newlyweds. For victims of disaster or the honors lists. For lady novelists. Or charity balls for the organizers of charity balls. This one's just for the family, with no dancers and no dance.

MARIE: No, don't tell him. It's better if he doesn't notice anything.

MARGUERITE: . . . and goes out like a light? That's impossible.

MARIE: You've no heart.

MARGUERITE: Oh, yes, I have! It's beating.

MARIE: You're inhuman.

[MARGUERITE: What does that mean?

MARIE: It's terrible,] he's not prepared.

MARGUERITE: It's your fault if he isn't. He's been like one of those travelers who linger at every inn, forgetting each time that the inn is not the end of the journey. When I reminded you that in life we must never forget our ultimate fate, you told me I was a pompous bluestocking.

JULIETTE (*aside*): It *is* pompous, too!

MARIE: As it's inevitable, at least he must be told as tactfully as possible. Tactfully, with great tact.

MARGUERITE: He ought always to have been prepared for it. He ought to have thought about it every day. The time he's wasted! (*To* JULIETTE:) What's the matter with you, goggling at us like that? You're not going to break down too, I hope. You can leave us; don't go too far away, we'll call you.

JULIETTE: So I don't have to sweep the living room now?

MARGUERITE: It's too late. Never mind. Leave us.

JULIETTE *goes out on the left.*

MARIE: Tell him gently, I implore you. Take your time. He might have a heart attack.

MARGUERITE: We haven't the time to take our time. This is the end of your happy days, your high jinks, your beanfeasts and your strip tease. It's all over. You've let things slide to the very last minute and now we've not a minute to lose. Obviously. It's the last. We've a few moments to do what ought to have been done over a period of years. I'll tell you when you have to leave us alone. Then, *I'll* help him.

MARIE: It's going to be so hard, so hard.

MARGUERITE: As hard for me as for you, and for him. Stop grizzling, I say! That's a piece of advice. That's an order.

MARIE: He won't do it.

MARGUERITE: Not at first.

MARIE: I'll hold him back.

MARGUERITE: Don't you dare! It's all got to take place decently. Let it be a success, a triumph. It's a long time since he had one. His palace is crumbling. His fields lie fallow. His mountains are sinking. The sea has broken the dikes and flooded the country. He's let it all go to rack and ruin. You've driven every thought from his mind with your perfumed embrace. Such bad taste! But that was him all over! Instead of conserving the soil, he's let acre upon acre plunge into the bowels of the earth.

MARIE: Expert advice on how to stop an earthquake!

MARGUERITE: I've no patience with you! . . . He could still have planted conifers in the sand and cemented the threatened areas. But no! Now the kingdom's as full of holes as a gigantic Gruyère cheese.

MARIE: We couldn't fight against fate, against a natural phenomenon like erosion.

MARGUERITE: Not to mention all those disastrous wars. While his drunken soldiers were sleeping it off, at night or after a lavish lunch in barracks, our neighbors were pushing back our frontier posts. Our national boundaries were shrinking. His soldiers didn't want to fight.

MARIE: They were conscientious objectors.

MARGUERITE: We called them conscientious objectors here at home. The victorious armies called them cowards and deserters, and they were shot. You can see the result: towns razed to the ground, burnt-out swimming pools, abandoned bistros. The young are leaving their homeland in hordes. At the start of his reign there were nine thousand million inhabitants.

MARIE: Too many. There wasn't room for them all.

MARGUERITE: And now only about a thousand old people left. Less. Even now, while I'm talking, they're passing away.

MARIE: There are forty-five *young* people too.

MARGUERITE: No one else wants *them*. *We* didn't want them either; we were forced to take them back. Anyway, they're aging fast. Repatriated at twenty-five, two days later and they're over eighty. You can't pretend that's the normal way to grow old.

MARIE: But the king, *he's* still young.

MARGUERITE: He *was* yesterday, he *was* last night. You'll see in a moment.

GUARD (*announcing*): His Notability, the Doctor, has returned. His Notability, His Notability!

The DOCTOR *enters through the large door on the right, which opens and closes by itself. He looks like an astrologer and an executioner at one and the same time. On his head he is wearing a pointed hat with stars. He is dressed in red with a hood hanging from the collar, and holding a great telescope.*

DOCTOR (*to* MARGUERITE): Good morning, your Majesty. (*To* MARIE:) Good morning, your Majesty. I hope your Majesties will forgive me for being rather late. I've come straight from the hospital, where I had to perform several surgical operations of the greatest import to science.

MARIE: You can't operate on the King!

MARGUERITE: You can't *now,* that's true.

DOCTOR (*looking at* MARGUERITE, *then at* MARIE): I know. Not his Majesty.

MARIE: Doctor, is there anything new? He *is* a little better, isn't he? Isn't he? He *could* show *some* improvement, couldn't he?

DOCTOR: He's in a typically critical condition that admits no change.

MARIE: It's true, there's no hope, no hope. (*Looking at* MARGUERITE.) She doesn't want me to hope, she won't allow it.

MARGUERITE: Many people have delusions of grandeur, but you're deluded by triviality. There's never been a queen like you! You make me ashamed for you. Oh! She's going to cry again.

DOCTOR: In point of fact, there *is,* if you like, *something* new to report.

MARIE: What's that?

DOCTOR: Something that merely confirms the previous symptoms. Mars and Saturn have collided.

MARGUERITE: As we expected.

DOCTOR: Both planets have exploded.

MARGUERITE: That's logical.

DOCTOR: The sun has lost between fifty and seventy-five percent of its strength.

MARGUERITE: That's natural.

DOCTOR: Snow is falling on the North Pole of the sun. The Milky Way seems to be curdling. The comet is exhausted, feeling its age, winding its tail around itself and curling up like a dying dog.

MARIE: It's not true, you're exaggerating. You must be. Yes, you're exaggerating.

DOCTOR: Do you wish to look through this telescope?

MARGUERITE (*to* DOCTOR): There's no point. We believe you. What else?

DOCTOR: Yesterday evening it was spring. It left us two hours and thirty minutes ago. Now it's November. Outside our frontiers, the grass is shooting up, the trees are turning green. All the cows are calving twice a day. Once in the morning and again in the afternoon about five, or a quarter past. Yet in our own country, the brittle leaves are peeling off. The trees are sighing and dying. The earth is quaking rather more than usual.

GUARD (*announcing*): The Royal Meteorological Institute calls attention to the bad weather conditions.

MARIE: I can feel the earth quaking, I can hear it. Yes, I'm afraid I really can.

MARGUERITE: It's that crack. It's getting wider, it's spreading.

DOCTOR: The lightning's stuck in the sky, the clouds are raining frogs, the thunder's mumbling. That's why we can't hear it. Twenty-five of our countrymen have been liquefied. Twelve have lost their heads. Decapitated. This time, without my surgical intervention.

MARGUERITE: Those are the signs all right.

DOCTOR: Whereas . . .

MARGUERITE (*interrupting him*): No need to go on. It's what always happens in a case like this. We know.

GUARD (*announcing*): His Majesty, the King!

Music.

Attention for His Majesty! Long live the King!

The KING *enters through the upstage door on the left. He has bare feet.* JULIETTE *comes in behind the* KING.

MARGUERITE: Now where has he scattered his slippers?

JULIETTE: Sire, they are here.

MARGUERITE: It's a bad habit to walk about barefoot.

MARIE (*to* JULIETTE): Put his slippers on. Hurry up! He'll catch cold!

MARGUERITE: It's no longer of any importance if he catches cold. It's just that it's a bad habit.

While JULIETTE *is putting the King's slippers on and*

MARIE *moves toward him, the royal music can still be heard.*

DOCTOR *(with a humble and unctuous bow)*: May I be allowed to wish your Majesty a good day. And my very best wishes.

MARGUERITE: That's nothing now but a hollow formality.

KING *(to* MARIE, *and then to* MARGUERITE): Good morning, Marie. Good morning, Marguerite. Still here? I mean, you're here already! How do you feel? *I* feel awful! I don't know quite what's wrong with me. My legs are a bit stiff. I had a job to get up, and my feet hurt! I must get some new slippers. Perhaps I've been growing! I had a bad night's sleep, what with the earth quaking, the frontiers retreating, the cattle bellowing and the sirens screaming. There's far too much noise. I really must look into it. We'll see what we can do. Ouch, my ribs! *(To* DOCTOR:) Good morning, Doctor. Is it lumbago? *(To the others:)* I'm expecting an engineer . . . from abroad. Ours are no good nowadays. They just don't care. Besides, we haven't any. Why did we close the Polytechnic? Oh yes! It fell through a hole in the ground. And why should we build more when they all disappear through a hole? On top of everything else, I've got a headache. And those clouds . . . I thought I'd banished the clouds. Clouds! We've had enough rain. Enough, I said! Enough rain. Enough, I said! Oh! Look at that! Off they go again! There's an idiotic cloud that can't restrain itself. Like an old man, weak in the bladder. *(To* JULIETTE:) What are you staring at me for? You look very red today. My bedroom's full of cobwebs. Go and brush them away.

JULIETTE: I removed them all while your Majesty was still

asleep. I can't think where they spring from. They keep on coming back.

DOCTOR (*to* MARGUERITE): You see, your Majesty. This, too, confirms my diagnosis.

KING (*to* MARIE): What's wrong with you, my love?

MARIE (*stammering*): I don't know . . . nothing . . . nothing wrong.

KING: You've got rings around your eyes. Have you been crying? Why?

MARIE: Oh God!

KING (*to* MARGUERITE): I won't have anyone upset her. And why did she say, "Oh God?"

MARGUERITE: It's an expression. (*To* JULIETTE:) Go and get rid of those cobwebs again.

KING: Oh yes! Those cobwebs, disgusting! They give you nightmares!

MARGUERITE (*to* JULIETTE): Hurry up, don't dawdle! Have you forgotten how to use a broom?

JULIETTE: Mine's all worn away. I need a new one. I could really do with twelve brooms.

JULIETTE *goes out.*

KING: Why are you all staring at me like this? Is there something abnormal about me? Now it's so normal to be abnormal, there's no such thing as abnormality. So that's straightened that out.

MARIE (*rushing toward the* KING): My dear King, you're limping!

KING (*taking two or three paces with a slight limp*): Limping? *I'm* not limping. I *am* limping a little.

MARIE: Your leg hurts. I'm going to help you along.

KING: It doesn't hurt. Why should it hurt? Why, yes, it *does* just a little. It's nothing. (*To* MARIE:) I don't need anyone to help me. Though I like being helped by you.

MARGUERITE (*moving toward the* KING): Sire, I have some news for you.

MARIE: No, be quiet!

MARGUERITE (*to* MARIE): Keep quiet yourself!

MARIE (*to the* KING): What she says isn't true.

KING: News about what? *What* isn't true? Marie, why do you look so sad! What's the matter with you?

MARGUERITE (*to the* KING): Sire, we have to inform you that you are going to die.

DOCTOR: Alas, yes, your Majesty.

KING: But I know that, of course I do! We *all* know it! You can remind me when the time comes. Marguerite, you have a mania for disagreeable conversation early in the morning.

MARGUERITE: It's midday already.

KING: It's not midday. Why yes, it is! It doesn't matter. For me, it's the morning. I haven't eaten anything yet. Let my breakfast be brought. To be honest, I'm not very hungry. Doctor, you'll have to give me some pills to stimulate my appetite and shake up my liver. My tongue's all coated, isn't it?

He shows his tongue to the DOCTOR.

DOCTOR: Yes, indeed, your Majesty.

KING: My liver's all choked up. I had nothing to drink last night, but I've a nasty taste in my mouth.

DOCTOR: Your Majesty, Queen Marguerite has spoken the truth. You *are* going to die.

KING: What, again? You get on my nerves! I'll die, yes, I'll die all right. In forty, fifty, three hundred years. Or even later. When I want to, when I've got the time, when I make up my mind. Meanwhile, let's get on with affairs of state. (*He climbs the steps of the throne.*) Ouch! My legs! My back! I've caught a cold. This palace is so badly heated, full of draughts and gales. What about those broken windowpanes? Have they replaced those tiles on the roof? No one works any more. I shall have to see to it myself, but I've had other things to do. You can't count on anyone. (*To* MARIE, *who is trying to support him:*) No, I can manage. (*He helps himself up with his scepter, using it as a stick.*) There's some use in this scepter yet. (*He manages to sit down, painfully, helped after all by* MARIE.) No, I say, no, I can do it. That's it! At last! This throne's got very hard! We ought to have it upholstered. And how is my country this morning?

MARGUERITE: What remains of it . . .

KING: There are still a few tidbits left. We've got to keep an eye on them, anyhow. And it'll give you something else to think about. Let us send for all our ministers.

JULIETTE *appears.*

Go and fetch the ministers. I expect they're still fast

asleep. They imagine there's no more work to be done.

JULIETTE: They've gone off on their holidays. Not very far, because now the country's all squashed up. It's shrunk. They're at the opposite end of the kingdom, in other words, just around the corner at the edge of the wood beside the stream. They've gone fishing. They hope to catch a few to feed the population.

KING: Go to the wood and fetch them.

JULIETTE: They won't come. They're off duty. But I'll go and see if you like. (*She goes to look through the window.*)

KING: No discipline!

JULIETTE: They've fallen into the stream.

MARIE: Try and fish them out again.

JULIETTE *goes out.*

KING: If the country could produce any other political experts, I'd give those two the sack.

MARIE: We'll find some more.

DOCTOR: We won't find any more, your Majesty.

MARGUERITE: You won't find any more, Berenger.

MARIE: Yes we will, among the school children, when they're grown up. We've a little time to wait, but once these two have been fished out, they can keep things going for a while.

DOCTOR: The only children you find in the schools today are a few congenital mental defectives, Mongoloids and hydrocephalics with goiters.

KING: I see the nation's not very fit. Try and cure them, Doctor, or improve their condition a bit. So at least they can learn the first four or five letters of the alphabet. In the old days, we used to kill them off.

DOCTOR: His Majesty could no longer allow himself that privilege! Or he'd have no more subjects left.

KING: Do something with them, anyway!

MARGUERITE: We can't improve anything now. We can't cure anyone. Even *you* are incurable now.

DOCTOR: Sire, you are now incurable.

KING: I am not ill.

MARIE: He feels quite well. (*To the* KING:) Don't you?

KING: A little stiffness, that's all. It's nothing. It's a lot better now, anyway.

MARIE: He says it's all right, you see, you see.

KING: Really, I feel fine.

MARGUERITE: You're going to die in an hour and a half, you're going to die at the end of the show.

KING: What did you say, my dear? That's not funny.

MARGUERITE: You're going to die at the end of the show.

MARIE: Oh God!

DOCTOR: Yes, Sire, you are going to die. You will not take your breakfast tomorrow morning. Nor will you dine tonight. The chef has shut off the gas. He's handing in his apron. He's putting the tablecloths and napkins away in the cupboard, forever.

MARIE: Don't speak so fast, don't speak so loud.

KING: And who can have given such orders, without my consent? I'm in good health. You're teasing me. Lies. (*To* MARGUERITE:) You've always wanted me dead. (*To* MARIE:) She's always wanted me dead. (*To* MARGUERITE:) I'll die when I want to. I'm the king. I'm the one to decide.

DOCTOR: You've lost the power to decide for yourself, your Majesty.

MARGUERITE: And now you can't even help falling ill.

KING: I'm *not* ill! (*To* MARIE:) Didn't you just say I wasn't ill? I'm still handsome.

MARGUERITE: And those pains of yours?

KING: All gone.

MARGUERITE: Move about a bit. You'll see!

KING (*who has just sat down again, tries to stand up*): Ouch! . . . That's because I wasn't mentally prepared. I didn't have time to think! I think and I am cured. The king can cure himself, but I was too engrossed in ruling my kingdom.

MARGUERITE: Your kingdom! What a state *that's* in! You can't govern it now. Really, you *know* you can't, but you won't admit it. You've lost your power now, over yourself and over the elements. You can't stop the rot and you've no more power over us.

MARIE: You'll always have power over me.

MARGUERITE: Not even you.

JULIETTE *enters.*

JULIETTE: It's too late to fish the ministers out now. The

stream they fell into, with all its banks and willows, has vanished into a bottomless pit.

KING: I see. It's a plot. You want me to abdicate.

MARGUERITE: That's the best way. A voluntary abdication.

DOCTOR: Abdicate, Sire. That would be best.

KING: Abdicate? Me?

MARGUERITE: Yes. Abdicate governmentally! And morally!

DOCTOR: And physically!

MARIE: Don't give your consent! Don't listen to them!

KING: They're mad. Or else they're traitors.

JULIETTE: Sire, Sire, my poor lord and master, Sire.

MARIE (*to the* KING): You must have them arrested.

KING (*to the* GUARD): Guard! Arrest them!

MARIE: Guard! Arrest them! (*To the* KING:) That's it. Give orders!

KING (*to the* GUARD): Arrest them all! Lock them up in the tower! No, the tower's collapsed. Take them away, and lock them up in the cellar, in the dungeons, or in the rabbit hutch. Arrest them, all of them! That's an order!

MARIE (*to the* GUARD): Arrest them!

GUARD (*without moving*): In the name of His Majesty . . . I . . . I . . . arrest . . . you.

MARIE (*to the* GUARD): Get moving, then!

JULIETTE: He's the one who's arrested.

KING (*to the* GUARD): Do it, then, Guard! Do it!

MARGUERITE: You see, now he can't move. He's got gout and rheumatism.

DOCTOR (*indicating the* GUARD): Sire, the army is paralyzed. An unknown virus has crept into his brain to sabotage his strong points.

MARGUERITE (*to the* KING): Your Majesty, you can see for yourself, it's your own orders that paralyze him.

MARIE (*to the* KING): Don't you believe it! She's trying to hypnotize you. [It's a question of will power. You can control the whole situation by will power.]

GUARD: I you . . . in the name of the King . . . I you . . . (*He stops speaking, his mouth wide open.*)

KING (*to the* GUARD): What's come over you? Speak! Advance! Do you think you're playing statues?

MARIE (*to the* KING): Don't ask him questions! Don't argue! Give orders! Sweep him off his feet in a whirlwind of will power!

DOCTOR: You see, your Majesty, he can't move a muscle. He can't say a word, he's turned to stone. He's deaf to you already. It's a characteristic symptom. Very pronounced, medically speaking.

KING: Now we'll see if I've still any power or not.

MARIE (*to the* KING): Prove that you have! You can if you want to.

KING: I'll prove that I want to, I'll prove I can.

MARIE: Stand up, first!

KING: I stand up. (*He makes a great effort, grimacing.*)

MARIE: You see how easy it is!

KING: You see, both of you, how easy it is! You're a pair
of humbugs! Conspirators, Bolsheviks! (*He walks to*
MARIE, *who tries to help him.*) No, no, alone . . .
because I can, all by myself.

He falls. JULIETTE *rushes forward to pick him up.*

I can get up by myself. (*He does indeed get up by
himself, but with difficulty.*)

GUARD: Long live the King!

The KING *falls down again.*

The King is dying.

MARIE: Long live the King!

The KING *stands up with difficulty, helping himself
with his scepter.*

GUARD: Long live the King!

The KING *falls down again.*

The King is dead!

MARIE: Long live the King! Long live the King!

MARGUERITE: What a farce!

The KING *stands up again, painfully.*

JULIETTE (*who has disappeared, reappears*): Long live the
King!

She disappears again. The KING *falls down again.*

GUARD: The King is dying!

MARIE: No! Long live the King! Stand up! Long live the
King!

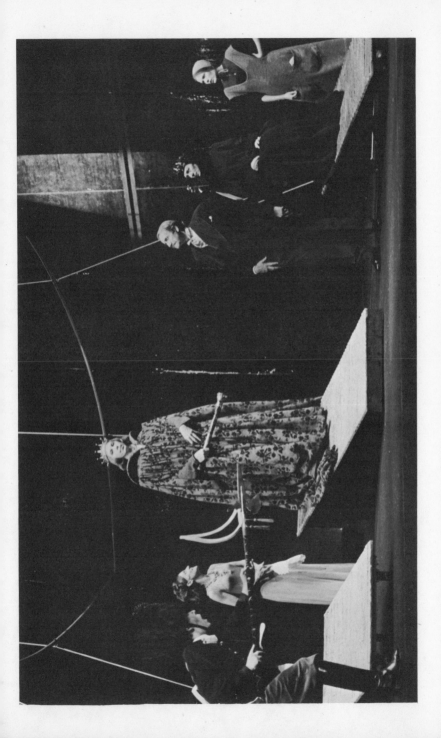

JULIETTE (*appearing, then disappearing again, while the* KING *stands up*): Long live the King!

This scene should be played like a tragic Punch and Judy show.

GUARD: Long live the King!

MARIE: You see, he's better now.

MARGUERITE: It's his last burst of energy, isn't it, Doctor?

DOCTOR (*to* MARGUERITE): Just a final effort before his strength gives out.

KING: I tripped, that's all. It can happen to anyone. It does happen, you know. My crown!

The crown had fallen to the ground when the KING *collapsed.* MARIE *puts it back on his head again.*

That's a bad omen.

MARIE: Don't you believe it!

The King's scepter falls.

KING: That's another bad omen.

MARIE: Don't you believe it! (*She gives him his scepter.*) Hold it firmly in your hand! Clench your fist!

GUARD: Long live . . . Long live . . . (*Then he falls silent.*)

DOCTOR (*to the* KING): Your Majesty . . .

MARGUERITE (*to the* DOCTOR, *indicating* MARIE): We must keep that woman quiet! She says anything that comes into her head. She's not to open her mouth again without our permission.

MARIE *is motionless.*

(*To the* DOCTOR, *indicating the* KING:) Now, try and make him understand.

DOCTOR (*to the* KING): Your Majesty, several decades or even three days ago, your empire was flourishing. In three days, you've lost all the wars you won. And those you lost, you've lost again. [While our harvests rotted in the fields and our continent became a desert, our neighbors' land turned green again. And it was a wilderness last Thursday!] The rockets you want to fire can't even get off the ground. Or else they leave the pad and drop back to earth with a thud.

KING: A technical fault.

DOCTOR: There weren't any in the past.

MARGUERITE: Your triumphs are all over. You've got to realize that.

DOCTOR: Your pains, your stiffness . . .

KING: I've never had them before. This is the first time.

DOCTOR: Exactly. That's the sign. It really has happened all at once, hasn't it?

MARGUERITE: You should have expected it.

DOCTOR: It's happened all at once and you're no longer your own master. You must have noticed, Sire. Try and have the courage to look facts in the face! Just try!

KING: I picked myself up. You're lying. I *did* pick myself up.

DOCTOR: You're a very sick man, and you could never make that effort again.

MARGUERITE: Of course not. It won't be long now. (*To the* KING:) What can you still *do*? Can you give an order that's obeyed? Can you change anything? Just try and you'll see.

KING: It's because I never used my will power that everything went to pieces. Sheer neglect. It can all be put right. It will all be restored and look like new. You'll soon see what I can do. Guard, move, approach!

MARGUERITE: He can't. He can only obey other people now. Guard, take two paces forward!

The GUARD *advances two paces.*

Guard, two paces back!

The GUARD *takes two paces back.*

KING: Off with that guard's head, off with his head!

The Guard's head leans a little to the right, a little to the left.

His head's toppling! It's going to fall!

MARGUERITE: No, it isn't. It wobbles a bit, that's all. No worse than it was before.

KING: Off with that doctor's head, off with it at once! Right now, off!

MARGUERITE: The Doctor has a sound head on his shoulders. He's got it screwed on all right!

DOCTOR: I'm sorry, Sire, as you see, I feel quite ashamed.

KING: Off with Marguerite's crown! Knock it on the floor!

It is the King's crown which again falls to the floor. MARGUERITE *picks it up.*

MARGUERITE: All right, I'll put it on again.

KING: Thank you. What *is* all this? Witchcraft? How have I lost my power over you? Don't imagine I'll let things go on like this. I'm going to get to the bottom of this. There must be rust in the machine. It stops the wheels from turning.

MARGUERITE (*to* MARIE): You can speak now. We give you permission.

MARIE (*to the* KING): Tell me to do something and I'll do it! Give me an order! Command me, Sire, command me! I'll obey you.

MARGUERITE (*to the* DOCTOR): She thinks what she calls love can achieve the impossible. Sentimental superstition. Things have changed. That's out of the question now. We're past that stage already. A long way past.

MARIE (*who has retreated backward to the left and is now near the window*): Your orders, my King. Your orders, my love. See how beautiful I am! Smell my perfume! Order me to come to you, to kiss you!

KING (*to* MARIE): Come to me, kiss me!

MARIE *does not move.*

Can you hear me?

MARIE: Why yes, I can hear you. I'll do it.

KING: Come to me, then!

MARIE: I'd like to. I'm going to. I want to do it. But my arms fall to my side.

KING: Dance, then!

MARIE *does not move.*

Dance! Or at least, turn your head, go to the window, open it and close it again!

MARIE: I can't!

KING: I expect you've got a stiff neck. You must have a stiff neck. Step forward, come closer to me!

MARIE: Yes, Sire.

KING: Come closer to me!

MARIE: Yes, Sire.

KING: And smile!

MARIE: I don't know what to do, how to walk. I've suddenly forgotten.

MARGUERITE: Take a few steps nearer!

MARIE *advances a little in the direction of the* KING.

KING: You see, she's coming!

MARGUERITE: Because she listened to *me.* (*To* MARIE:) Stop! Stand still!

MARIE: Forgive me, your Majesty. It's not my fault.

MARGUERITE (*to the* KING): Do you need any more proof?

KING: I order trees to sprout from the floor. (*Pause.*) I order the roof to disappear. (*Pause.*) What? Nothing? I order rain to fall. (*Pause—still nothing happens.*) I order a thunderbolt, one I can hold in my hand. (*Pause.*) I order leaves to grow again. (*He goes to the window.*) What? Nothing? I order Juliette to come in through the great door.

JULIETTE *comes in through the small door upstage left.*

Not that way, this way! Go out by that door. (*He indicates the large door.*)

JULIETTE *goes out by the small door on the left, opposite.*

(*To* JULIETTE:) I order you to stay.

JULIETTE *has gone out.*

I order bugles to sound. I order bells to ring! A salute from a hundred and twenty-one guns in my honor. (*He listens.*) Nothing! . . . Wait! Yes! . . . I can hear something.

DOCTOR: It's only the buzzing in your ears, your Majesty.

MARGUERITE (*to the* KING): Don't try any more! You're making a fool of yourself.

MARIE (*to the* KING): You're—you're getting too tired, my dear little King. Don't despair! You're soaked in perspiration. Rest a little! After a while, we'll start again. Wait for an hour and then we'll manage it.

MARGUERITE (*to the* KING): In one hour and twenty-five minutes, you're going to die.

DOCTOR: Yes, Sire. In one hour, twenty-four minutes and fifty seconds.

KING (*to* MARIE): Marie!

MARGUERITE: In one hour, twenty-four minutes and forty-one seconds. (*To the* KING:) Prepare yourself!

MARIE: Don't give in!

MARGUERITE (*to* MARIE): Stop trying to distract him! [Don't open your arms to him! He's slipping away already.]

You can't hold him back now. The official program must be followed, in every detail.

GUARD (*announcing*): The ceremony is about to commence!

General commotion. They all take up their positions, as if for some solemn ceremony. The KING *is seated on his throne, with* MARIE *at his side.*

KING: Let time turn back in its tracks.

MARIE: Let us be as we were twenty years ago.

KING: Let it be last week.

MARIE: Let it be yesterday evening. Turn back, time! Turn back! Time, stop!

MARGUERITE: There is no more time. Time has melted in his hands.

DOCTOR (*to* MARGUERITE, *after looking heavenward through his telescope*): If you look through this telescope, which can see through roofs and walls, you will notice a gap in the sky that used to house the Royal Constellation. In the annals of the universe, his Majesty has been entered as deceased.

GUARD: The King is dead! Long live the King!

MARGUERITE (*to the* GUARD): Idiot! Can't you keep quiet!

DOCTOR: He is, indeed, far more dead than alive.

KING: I'm not. I don't want to die. Please don't let me die! Be kind to me, all of you, don't let me die! I don't want to.

[MARIE (*helplessly*): How can I give him the strength to resist? I'm weakening, myself. He doesn't believe *me* any more, he only believes *them*. (*To the* KING:) But don't give up hope, there's still hope!

MARGUERITE (*to* MARIE): Don't confuse him! You'll only make things worse for him now.]

KING: I don't want to, I don't want to.

DOCTOR: The crisis I was expecting. It's perfectly normal. The first breach in his defenses, already.

MARGUERITE (*to* MARIE): The crisis will pass.

GUARD (*announcing*): The King is passing!

DOCTOR: We shall miss your Majesty greatly! And we shall say so publicly. That's a promise.

KING: I don't want to die.

MARIE: Oh dear, look! His hair has suddenly gone white.

The King's hair has indeed turned white. The wrinkles are spreading across his forehead, over his face. All at once, he looks fourteen centuries older.

DOCTOR: Antiquated. And so suddenly, too!

KING: Kings ought to be immortal.

MARGUERITE: They are. Provisionally.

KING: They promised me *I* could choose the time when I would die.

MARGUERITE: That's because they thought you'd have chosen long ago. But you acquired a taste for authority. Now you must be *made* to choose. You got stuck in the mud of life. You felt warm and cozy. (*Sharply.*) Now you're going to freeze.

KING: I've been trapped. I should have been warned, I've been trapped.

MARGUERITE: You were often warned.

KING: You warned me too soon. I won't die. . . . I don't want to. Someone must save me, as I can't save myself.

MARGUERITE [It's your fault if you've been taken unawares, you ought to have been prepared. You never had the time.] You'd been condemned, and you should have thought about that the very first day, and then day after day, five minutes every day. It wasn't much to give up. Five minutes every day. Then ten minutes, a quarter, half an hour. That's the way to train yourself.

KING: I *did* think about it.

MARGUERITE: Not seriously, not profoundly, never with all your heart and soul.

MARIE: He was alive.

MARGUERITE: Too much alive. (*To the* KING:) You ought to have had this thought permanently at the back of your mind.

DOCTOR: He never looked ahead, he's always lived from day to day, like most people.

MARGUERITE: You kept on putting it off. At twenty you said you'd wait till your fortieth year before you went into training. At forty . . .

KING: I was in such good health, I was so young!

MARGUERITE: At forty: why not wait till you were fifty? At fifty . . .

KING: I was full of life, wonderfully full of life!

MARGUERITE: At fifty, you wanted first to reach your sixties. And so you went on, from sixty to ninety to a hundred and twenty-five to two hundred, until you were four hundred years old. Instead of putting things off for ten years at a time, you put them off for fifty. Then you postponed them from century to century.

KING: But I was just about to start. Oh! If I could have a whole century before me, perhaps then I'd have time!

DOCTOR: All you have now is one hour, Sire. You must do it all in an hour.

MARIE: He'll never have enough time, it's impossible. He must be given more.

MARGUERITE: That *is* impossible. But an hour gives him all the time he needs.

DOCTOR: A well spent hour's better than whole centuries of neglect and failure. Five minutes are enough, ten fully conscious seconds. We're giving him an hour! Sixty minutes, three thousand and six hundred seconds. He's in luck.

MARGUERITE: He's lingered too long by the wayside.

[MARIE: We've been ruling the kingdom. *He's* been working.

GUARD: The Labors of Hercules.

MARGUERITE: Pottering about.]

Enter JULIETTE.

JULIETTE: Poor Majesty, my poor master's been playing truant.

KING: I'm like a schoolboy who hasn't done his homework and sits for an exam without swatting up the papers.

MARGUERITE: Don't let that worry you!

KING: . . . like an actor on the first night who doesn't know his lines and who dries, dries, dries. Like an orator pushed onto a platform who's forgotten his speech and has no idea who he's meant to be addressing. I don't know this audience, and I don't want to. I've nothing to say to them. What a state I'm in!

GUARD (*announcing*): The King has just alluded to his State.

MARGUERITE: A state of ignorance.

JULIETTE: He'd like to go on playing truant for centuries to come.

KING: I'd like to re-sit the exam.

MARGUERITE: You'll take it now. No re-sits are allowed.

DOCTOR: There's nothing you can do, your Majesty. Neither can we. We only practice medical science, we can't perform miracles.

KING: Do the people know the news? Have you warned them? I want everyone to know that the King is going to die. (*He makes a rush to open the window, with a great effort, for his limp is getting worse.*) My good people, I am going to die! Hear me! Your King is going to die!

MARGUERITE (*to the* DOCTOR): They mustn't hear him. Stop him shouting!

KING: Hands off the King! I want everyone to know I'm going to die! (*He shouts.*)

DOCTOR: Scandalous!

KING: People, I've got to die!

MARGUERITE: What was once a king is now a pig that's being slaughtered.

MARIE: He's just a king. He's just a man.

DOCTOR: Your Majesty, think of the death of Louis XIV, of Philip II, or of the Emperor Charles V, who slept in his own coffin for twenty years. It is your Majesty's duty to die with dignity.

KING: Die with dignity? (*At the window.*) Help! Your King is going to die!

MARIE: Poor dear King, my poor little King!

JULIETTE: Shouting won't help.

A feeble echo can be heard in the distance: "The King is going to die."

KING: Hear that?

MARIE: I hear, I can hear.

KING: They've answered me. Perhaps they're going to save me.

JULIETTE: There's no one there.

The echo can be heard: "Help!"

DOCTOR: It's only the echo, a bit late in answering.

MARGUERITE: Late as usual, like everything else in this country. Nothing functions properly.

KING (*leaving the window*): It's impossible. (*Going back to the window:*) I'm frightened. It's impossible.

MARGUERITE: He imagines no one's ever died before.

MARIE: No one *has* died before.

MARGUERITE: It's all very painful.

JULIETTE: He's crying! Just like anyone else!

MARGUERITE: What a commonplace reaction! I hoped terror
would have produced some fine ringing phrases. (*To
the* DOCTOR:) I must put you in charge of the chron-
icles. We'll attribute to him the fine words spoken by
others. We'll invent some new ones, if need be.

DOCTOR: We'll credit him with some edifying maxims. (*To*
MARGUERITE:) We'll watch over his legend. (*To the*
KING:) We'll watch over your legend, your Majesty.

KING (*at the window*): People, help! . . . Help, people!

MARGUERITE: Haven't you had enough, your Majesty? It's
a waste of effort.

KING (*at the window*): Who will give me his life? Who will
give his life for the King's? His life for the good old
King's, his life for the poor old King's?

MARGUERITE: It's indecent!

MARIE: Let him try everything once.

JULIETTE: As there's no one left in the country to hear,
why not? (*She goes out.*)

[MARGUERITE: The spies are still with us.

DOCTOR: Enemy ears listening at the frontiers.

MARGUERITE: He'll disgrace us all, panicking like this.]

DOCTOR: The echo's stopped answering. His voice doesn't

carry any more. He can shout as much as he likes. It won't even reach as far as the garden wall.

MARGUERITE (*while the* KING *is wailing*): He's moaning.

DOCTOR: We're the only ones who can hear him now. He can't even hear himself.

The KING *turns around and takes a few steps toward the center of the stage.*

KING: I'm cold, I'm frightened, I'm crying.

MARIE: His legs are all stiff.

DOCTOR: He's riddled with rheumatism. (*To* MARGUERITE:) An injection to quiet him?

JULIETTE *appears with an invalid chair on wheels, which has a crown and royal emblems on the back.*

KING: I won't have an injection.

MARIE: No injection.

KING: I know what they mean! I've had injections given to other people before! (*To* JULIETTE:) I never told you to bring that chair. I'm going for a walk, I want to take the air.

JULIETTE *leaves the chair in a corner of the stage on the left and goes out.*

MARGUERITE: Sit down in that chair or you'll fall.

The KING *is, in fact, staggering.*

KING: I won't give in! I intend to stay on my feet.

JULIETTE *returns with a blanket.*

JULIETTE: You'd feel much better, Sire, much more com-

fortable with a blanket over your knees and a hot water bottle. (*She goes out.*)

KING: No, I want to stay on my feet. I want to scream. I want to scream. (*He screams.*)

GUARD (*announcing*): His Majesty is screaming!

DOCTOR (*to* MARGUERITE): He won't scream for long. I know the symptoms. He'll get tired. He'll stop and then he'll listen to us.

JULIETTE *comes in, bringing more warm clothing and a hot water bottle.*

KING (*to* JULIETTE): I won't have them!

MARGUERITE: Sit down quickly, sit down.

KING: I refuse! (*He tries to climb the steps of the throne and fails. He goes and sits down all the same, collapsing on the Queen's throne to the right.*) I can't help it, I nearly fell over.

JULIETTE, *after following the* KING *with the objects mentioned above, goes and puts them on the invalid chair.*

MARGUERITE (*to* JULIETTE): Take his scepter, it's too heavy for him.

KING (*to* JULIETTE, *who is returning to him with a nightcap*): I won't wear that!

JULIETTE: It's a sort of crown, but not so heavy.

KING: Let me keep my scepter!

MARGUERITE: You've no longer the strength to hold it.

DOCTOR: It's no good trying to lean on it now. We'll carry you. We'll wheel you along in the chair.

KING: I want to keep it.

MARIE (*to* JULIETTE): Leave him his scepter! He wants it.

JULIETTE *looks to* MARGUERITE *for her instructions.*

MARGUERITE: After all, I don't see why not.

JULIETTE *gives the scepter back to the* KING.

KING: Perhaps it's not true. Tell me it's not true. Perhaps it's a nightmare.

The others are silent.

Perhaps there's a ten to one chance, one chance in a thousand.

The others are silent. The KING *is sobbing.*

I often used to win the sweepstakes!

DOCTOR: Your Majesty!

KING: I can't listen to you any more, I'm too frightened. (*He is sobbing and moaning.*)

MARGUERITE: You must listen, Sire.

KING: I *won't* hear what you're saying. Your words frighten me. I won't hear any more talk. (*To* MARIE, *who is trying to approach him:*) Don't you come any nearer either. You frighten me with your pity. (*He moans again.*)

[MARIE: He's like a small child. He's a little boy again.

MARGUERITE: An ugly little boy, with a beard and wrinkles. You're too lenient with him!

JULIETTE (*to* MARGUERITE): You don't try and put yourself in his place.]

KING: No, speak to me! I didn't mean it, speak to me! Stand by me, hold me! Help me up! No, I want to run away. (*He rises painfully to his feet and goes to sit down on the other small throne on the left.*)

JULIETTE: His legs can hardly carry him.

KING: It hurts to move my arms, too. Does that mean it's starting? No. Why was I born if it wasn't forever? Damn my parents! What a joke, what a farce! I came into the world five minutes ago. I got married three minutes ago.

MARGUERITE: Two hundred and eighty-three years.

KING: I came to the throne two and a half minutes ago.

MARGUERITE: Two hundred and seventy-seven years and three months.

KING: Never had time to say knife! Never had time to get to know life.

MARGUERITE: He never even tried.

MARIE: It was like a brisk walk through a flowery lane, a promise that's broken, a smile that fades.

MARGUERITE (*to the* DOCTOR, *continuing*): Yet he had the greatest experts to tell him all about it. Theologians, people of experience, and books he never read.

KING: I never had the time.

MARGUERITE: You used to say you had all the time in the world.

KING: I never had the time, I never had the time, I never had the time!

[JULIETTE: He's going back to that again.

MARGUERITE (*to the* DOCTOR): All the time it's the same old story.]

DOCTOR: I'd say things were looking up. However much he moans and groans, he's started to reason things out. He's complaining, protesting, expressing himself. That means he's begun to resign himself.

KING: I shall never resign myself.

DOCTOR: As he says he won't, it's a sign that he *will*. He's posing the problem of resignation, raising the question.

MARGUERITE: At last!

DOCTOR: Your Majesty, you have made war one hundred and eighty times. You have led your armies into two thousand battles. First, on a white horse with a conspicuous red-and-white plume, and you never knew fear. Then, when you modernized the army, you would stand on top of a tank, or on the wing of a fighter plane leading the formation.

MARIE: He was a hero.

DOCTOR: You have come near death a thousand times.

KING: I only came *near* it. I could tell it wasn't meant for me.

MARIE: You were a hero, do you hear? Remember that.

MARGUERITE: Aided and abetted by this doctor here, the executioner, you ordered the assassination . . .

KING: Execution, not assassination.

DOCTOR (*to* MARGUERITE): Execution, your Majesty, not assassination. I was only obeying orders. I was a mere instrument, just an executor, not an executioner. It was all euthanasia to me. Anyhow, I'm sorry. Please forgive me.

MARGUERITE (*to the* KING): I tell you, you had my parents butchered, your own brothers, your rivals, our cousins and great-grandcousins, and all their families, friends and cattle. You massacred the lot and scorched all their lands.

DOCTOR: His Majesty used to say they were going to die one day, anyway.

KING: That was for reasons of State.

MARGUERITE: You're dying too because of your state.

KING: But I *am* the State.

JULIETTE: And what a state the poor man's in!

MARIE: He was the law, above the law.

[KING: I'm not the law any more.

DOCTOR: He admits it. Better and better.

MARGUERITE: That makes things easier.]

KING (*groaning*): I'm not above the law any more, not above the law any more.

GUARD (*announcing*): The King is no more above the law.

JULIETTE: The poor old boy's no more above the law. He's just like us and not unlike my granddad!

MARIE: Poor little chap, poor child!

KING: Child! A child? Then I can make a fresh start! I want to start again. (*To* MARIE:) I want to be a baby and you can be my mother. Then they won't come for me. I still don't know my reading, writing and arithmetic. I want to go back to school and be with all my playmates. What do two and two make?

JULIETTE: Two and two make four.

MARGUERITE (*to the* KING): You knew that already.

KING: She was only prompting me. . . . Oh dear, it's no good trying to cheat! Oh dear, oh dear! There are so many people being born at this moment, numberless babies all over the world.

MARGUERITE: Not in *our* country.

DOCTOR: The birth rate's down to zero.

JULIETTE: Not a lettuce, not a grass that grows.

MARGUERITE: Utter sterility, because of you!

MARIE: I won't have you blaming him!

JULIETTE: Perhaps everything will grow again.

MARGUERITE: When he's accepted the inevitable. When he's gone.

KING: When I've gone, when I've gone. They'll laugh and stuff themselves silly and dance on my tomb. As if I'd never existed. Oh, please make them all remember me! Make them weep and despair and perpetuate my memory in all their history books. Make everyone learn my life by heart. Make them all live it again. Let the schoolchildren and the scholars study nothing else but me, my kingdom and my exploits. Let them burn all the other books, destroy all the statues and set mine up in all the public squares. My portrait in every Ministry, my photograph in every office of every Town Hall, including Rates and Taxes, and in *all* the hospitals. Let every car and pushcart, flying ship and steamplane be named after me. Make them forget all other captains and kings, poets, tenors and philosophers, and fill every conscious mind with memories of me. Let them learn to read by spelling out my name: B, E, BE for Berenger. Let my likeness be on all the ikons, me on the millions of crosses in all our churches. Make them say Mass for me and let *me* be the Host. Let all the windows light up in the shape and color of my eyes. And the rivers trace my profile on the plains! Let them cry my name throughout eternity, and beg me and implore me.

MARIE: Perhaps you'll come back again?

KING: Perhaps I will come back. Let them preserve my body in some palace, on a throne, and let them bring me food. Let musicians play for me and virgins grovel at my ice-cold feet.

The KING has risen in order to make this speech.

JULIETTE (*to* MARGUERITE): He's raving, Ma'am.

GUARD (*announcing*): His Majesty the King is delirious.

MARGUERITE: Not yet. There's too much sense in what he says. Too much, and not enough.

DOCTOR (*to the* KING): If such be your will, your Majesty, we will embalm your body and preserve it.

JULIETTE: As long as we can.

KING: Horror! I don't want to be embalmed. I want nothing to do with that corpse. I don't want to be burnt. I don't want to be buried, I don't want to be thrown to the wild beasts or the vultures. I want to feel arms around me, warm arms, cool arms, soft arms, strong arms.

JULIETTE: He's not too sure what he *does* want.

MARGUERITE: We'll make his mind up for him. (*To* MARIE:) Now don't faint!

JULIETTE *is weeping*.

And there's another one! They're always the same!

KING: If I *am* remembered, I wonder for how long? Let them remember me to the end of time. And beyond the end of time, in twenty thousand years, in two hundred and fifty-five thousand million years . . . There'll be no one left to think of anyone then. They'll forget before that. Selfish, the lot of them. They only think of their own little lives, of their own skins. Not of *mine*. If the whole earth's going to wear out or melt away, it will. If every universe is going to explode, explode it will. It's all the same whether it's tomorrow or in countless centuries to come. What's got to finish one day is finished now.

MARGUERITE: Everything is yesterday.

JULIETTE: Even "today" will be "yesterday."

DOCTOR: All things pass into the past.

MARIE: My darling King, there is no past, there is no future. Remember, there's only a present that goes right on to the end, everything is present. Be present, be the present!

KING: Alas! I'm only present in the past.

MARIE: No, you're not.

MARGUERITE: That's right, Berenger, try and get things straight.

MARIE: Yes, my King, get things straight, my darling! Stop torturing yourself! "Exist" and "die" are just words, figments of our imagination. Once you realize that, nothing can touch you. [Forget our empty clichés. We can never know what it really means, "exist" or "die." Or if we think we do, our knowledge has deceived us. Stand firm, get a grip on yourself! Never lose sight of yourself again! Sweep everything else into oblivion! *Now* you exist, you *are*. Forget the rest. That's the only truth.] Just be an eternal question mark: what ...? why ...? how ...? And remember: that you can't find the answers is an answer in itself. It's you, all the life in you, straining to break out. Dive into an endless maze of wonder and surprise, then you too will have no end, and can exist forever. Everything is strange and undefinable. Let it dazzle and confound you! Tear your prison bars aside and batter down the walls! Escape from definitions and you will breathe again!

DOCTOR: He's choking!

MARGUERITE: Fear cramps his vision.

MARIE: Open the floodgates of joy and light to dazzle and confound you. Illuminating waves of joy will fill your veins with wonder. If you want them to.

JULIETTE: You bet he does.

MARIE (*in a tone of supplication*): I implore you to remember that morning in June we spent together by the sea, when happiness raced through you and inflamed you. You knew then what joy meant: rich, changeless and undying. If you knew it once, you can know it now. You found that fiery radiance within you. If it *was* there *once,* it is *still* there *now.* Find it again. Look for it, in yourself.

KING: I don't understand.

MARIE: You don't understand any more.

MARGUERITE: He never did understand himself.

MARIE: Pull yourself together!

KING: How do I manage that? No one can or will help me. And *I* can't help myself. Oh help me, sun! Sun, chase away the shadows and hold back the night! Sun, sun, illumine every tomb, shine into every hole and corner, every nook and cranny! Creep deep inside me! Ah! Now my feet are turning cold. Come and warm me, pierce my body, steal beneath my skin, and blaze into my eyes! Restore their failing light, and let me see, see, see! Sun, sun, will you miss me? Good little sun, protect me! And if you're in need of some small sacrifice, then parch and wither up the world. Let every human creature die provided *I* can live forever, even alone in a limitless desert. I'll come to terms with solitude. I'll keep alive the memory of others, and I'll miss them quite sincerely. But I can live in the void, in a vast and airy wasteland. It's better to miss one's friends than to be missed oneself. Besides, one never is. Light of our days, come and save me!

DOCTOR (*to* MARIE): This is not the light *you* meant. [This is not the timeless waste you wanted him to aim for: He didn't understand you, it's too much for his poor brain.]

MARGUERITE (*to* MARIE, *or referring to* MARIE): Love's labors lost. You're on the wrong track.

KING: Let me go on living century after century, even with a raging toothache. But I fear what must end one day ·has ended now.

[DOCTOR: Well, Sire, what are you waiting for?]

MARGUERITE: It's only his speeches that are never ending! (*Indicating* MARIE *and* JULIETTE.) And these two weeping women. They only push him deeper in the mire, trap him, bind him and hold him up.

KING: No, there's not enough weeping, not enough lamentation. Not enough anguish. (*To* MARGUERITE:) Don't stop them weeping and wailing and pitying their King, their young King, old King, poor little King. *I* feel pity when I think how they'll miss me, never see me again, and be left behind all alone. I'm still the one who thinks about others, about everyone. All the rest of you, be me, come inside me, come beneath my skin. I'm dying, you hear, I'm trying to tell you. I'm dying, but I can't express it, unless I talk like a book and make literature of it.

[MARGUERITE: Is that what·it is!

DOCTOR: It's not worth recording his words. Nothing new.

KING: They're all strangers to me. I thought they were my family. I'm frightened, I'm sinking, I'm drowning, I've gone blank, I've never existed. I'm dying.

MARGUERITE: Now that *is* literature!]

DOCTOR: And that's the way it goes on, to the bitter end. As long as we live we turn everything into literature.

MARIE: If only it could console him!

GUARD (*announcing*): The King finds some consolation in literature!

KING: No, no. I know, nothing can console me. It just wells up inside me, then drains away. Oh dear, oh dear, oh dear, oh dear, oh dear! (*Lamentations—then without declamation, he goes on moaning gently to himself.*) Help me, you countless thousands who died before me! Tell me how you managed to accept death and die. Then teach me! Let your example be a consolation to me, let me lean on you like crutches, like a brother's arms. Help me to cross the threshold you have crossed! Come back from the other side a while and help me! Assist me, you who were frightened and did not want to go! What was it like? Who held you up? Who dragged you there, who pushed you? Were you afraid to the very end? And you who were strong and courageous, who accepted death with indifference and serenity, teach me your indifference and serenity, teach me resignation!

The following dialogue should be spoken and acted as though it were ritual, with solemnity, almost chanted, accompanied by various movements, with the actors kneeling, holding out their arms, etc.

JULIETTE: You statues, you dark or shining phantoms, ancients and shades . . .

MARIE: Teach him serenity.   *unclouded, bright*

GUARD: Teach him indifference.   *have no marked feel one way or the other*

DOCTOR: Teach him resignation.   *acceptance*

MARGUERITE: Make him see reason and set his mind at rest.

KING: You suicides, teach me how to feel disgust for life!
Teach me lassitude!, What drug must I take for that?

exhaustion – I want to be taught

DOCTOR: I could prescribe euphoric pills or tranquilizers.

MARGUERITE: He'd vomit them up!

JULIETTE: You remembrances . . .

GUARD: You pictures of days gone by . . .

JULIETTE: . . . which no longer exist but in our memories
of memories . . .

GUARD: Recollections of recollections . . .

MARGUERITE: He's got to learn how to let go and then
surrender completely.

GUARD: . . . we invoke you.

MARIE: You morning mists and dews . . .

JULIETTE: You evening smoke and clouds . . .

MARIE: You saints, you wise and foolish virgins, help him!
For *I* cannot.

JULIETTE: Help him!

KING: You who died blissfully, who looked death in the
face, who remained conscious of your end . . .

JULIETTE: Help him!

MARIE: Help him all of you, help him, I beg you!

KING: You who died happy, what face did you see close to
yours? What smile gave you ease and made *you* smile?
What were the last rays of light that brushed your
face?

JULIETTE: Help him, you thousand millions of the dead!

GUARD: Oh you, great Nothing, help the King!

KING: Thousands and millions of the dead. They multiply my anguish. I am the dying agony of all. My death is manifold. So many worlds will flicker out in me.

MARGUERITE: Life is exile.

KING: I know, I know.

DOCTOR: In short, Majesty, you will return to your own country.

MARIE: You'll go back where you came from when you were born. Don't be so frightened, you're sure to find something familiar there.

[KING: I like exile. I ran away from my homeland and I don't want to go back. What *was* that world like?

MARGUERITE: Try and remember.

KING: I can see nothing, I can see nothing.

MARGUERITE: Remember! Come along, think! Think carefully! Think, just think! You've never thought!

DOCTOR: He's never given it a second thought since then!]

MARIE: Other world, lost world, buried and forgotten world, rise again from the deep!

JULIETTE: Other plains, other valleys, other mountain chains . . .

MARIE: Remind them of your name.

[KING: No memories of that distant land.

JULIETTE: He can't remember his homeland.

DOCTOR: He's in no state to do so, he's too weak.

KING: No nostalgia, however dim or fleeting.]

MARGUERITE: Plunge into your memories, dive through the gaps in your memory into a world beyond memory. (*To the* DOCTOR:) *This* is the only world he really misses!

MARIE: Memories immemorial, appear before him! Help him!

[DOCTOR: You see, it's quite a problem to get him to take the plunge.

MARGUERITE: He'll have to do it.

GUARD: His Majesty's never been down in a diving bell.

JULIETTE: Pity he never had the training.

MARGUERITE: It's a job he'll have to learn.]

KING: When faced with death, even a little ant puts up a fight. Suddenly, he's all alone, torn from his companions. In him, too, the universe flickers out. It's not natural to die, because no one ever wants to. I want to exist.

JULIETTE: That's all he knows. He wants to exist forever.

[MARIE: It seems to him he always *has.*

MARGUERITE: He'll have to stop looking about him, stop clinging to pictures of the outside world. He must shut himself up and lock himself in. (*To the* KING:) Not another word, be quiet, stay inside! Stop looking around and it'll do you good!

KING: Not the sort of good *I* want.

DOCTOR (*to* MARGUERITE): We haven't quite got to that stage. He still can't manage that. Your Majesty should

encourage him, of course, but don't push him too far
—not yet.

MARGUERITE: It won't be easy, but we can be patient and
wait.

DOCTOR: We're sure of the final result.]

KING: Doctor, Doctor, am I in the throes of death already?
. . . No, you've made a mistake . . . not yet . . . not yet.
(*A kind of sigh of relief.*) It hasn't started yet. I exist,
I'm still here. I can see. There are walls and furniture
here, there's air to breathe, I can watch people watching me and catch their voices. I'm alive, I can think, I
can see, I can hear, I can still see and hear. A fanfare!

*A sort of fanfare can be heard far away in the distance.
He starts walking.*

GUARD: The King is walking! Long live the King!

The KING *falls down.*

JULIETTE: He's down!

GUARD: The King is down! The King is dying!

The KING *gets up.*

MARIE: He's up again!

GUARD: The King is up! Long live the King!

MARIE: He's up again!

GUARD: Long live the King!

The KING *falls down.*

The King is dead!

MARIE: He's up again!

The KING *does indeed get up again.*

He's still alive!

GUARD: Long live the King!

The KING *makes for his throne.*

JULIETTE: He wants to sit on his throne.

MARIE: The King still reigns! The King still reigns!

DOCTOR: And now for the delirium.

MARIE (*to the* KING, *who is trying to totter up the steps of his throne*): Don't let go, hang on! (*To* JULIETTE, *who is trying to help the* KING:) Leave him alone! He can do it alone!

The KING *fails to climb the steps of the throne.*

[KING: And yet I've still got my legs!

MARIE: Try again!]

MARGUERITE: We've got thirty-two minutes and thirty seconds left.

KING: I can still stand up.

DOCTOR (*to* MARGUERITE): It's the last convulsion but one.

The KING *falls into the invalid chair, which* JULIETTE *has just brought forward. They cover him up and give him a hot water bottle, while he is still saying:*

KING: I can still stand up.

The hot water bottle, the blankets, etc., are gradually brought into the following scene by JULIETTE.

MARIE: You're out of breath, you're tired. Have a rest and you can stand up again later.

MARGUERITE (*to* MARIE): Don't lie! That doesn't help him!

KING (*in his chair*): I used to like Mozart. I'll never hear that music again.

MARGUERITE: You'll forget all about it.

KING (*to* JULIETTE): Did you mend my trousers? Or do you think now it's not worth the trouble? There was a hole in my red cloak. Have you patched it? Have you sewn those buttons on my pajamas? Have you had my shoes resoled?

JULIETTE: I never gave it another thought.

KING: You never gave it another thought! What *do* you think about? Talk to me! What does your husband do?

JULIETTE *has now put on, or is putting on, her nurse's cap and white apron.*

JULIETTE: I'm a widow.

KING: What do you think about when you do the housework?

JULIETTE: Nothing, your Majesty.

KING: Where do you come from? What's your family?

MARGUERITE (*to the* KING): You never took any interest before.

MARIE: He's never had time to ask her.

MARGUERITE (*to the* KING): And you're not really interested now.

DOCTOR: He wants to gain time.

KING (*to* JULIETTE): Tell me how you live. What sort of life do you have?

JULIETTE: A bad life, Sire.

KING: Life can never be bad. It's a contradiction in terms.

JULIETTE: Life's not very beautiful.

KING: Life is life.

JULIETTE: When I get up in the winter, it's still dark. And I'm cold as ice.

KING: So am I. But it's not the same cold. You don't like feeling cold?

JULIETTE: When I get up in the summer, it's only just beginning to get light. A pale sort of light.

KING (*rapturously*): A *pale* light! There are all sorts of light: blue and pink and white and green, and *pale!*

JULIETTE: I do all the palace laundry in the wash house. It hurts my hands and cracks my skin.

KING (*rapturously*): And it hurts! One can feel one's skin! Haven't they bought you a washing machine yet? Marguerite! A palace, and no washing machine!

MARGUERITE: We had to pawn it to raise a State loan.

JULIETTE: I empty the chamber pots. I make the beds.

KING: She makes the beds! Where we lie down and go to sleep and then wake up again. Did you ever realize that every day you woke up? To wake up every day . . . Every morning one comes into the world.

JULIETTE: I polish the parquet floors, and sweep, sweep, sweep! There's no end to it.

KING (*rapturously*): There's no end to it!

JULIETTE: It gives me the backache.

KING: That's right. She has a back! We've all got backs!

JULIETTE: Pains in the kidneys.

KING: And kidneys too!

JULIETTE: And now we've no gardeners left, I dig and rake and sow.

KING: And then things grow!

JULIETTE: I get quite worn out, exhausted!

KING: You ought to have told us.

JULIETTE: I *did* tell you.

KING: That's true. Such a lot has escaped my notice. [I never got to know everything. I never went everywhere I could. My life could have been so full.]

JULIETTE: There's no window in my room.

KING (*rapturously again*): No window! You go out in search of light. You find it and then you smile. To go out, you turn the key in the door, open it, then close it again and turn the key to lock it. Where do you live?

JULIETTE: In the attic.

KING: To come down in the morning, you take the stairs, you go down one step, then another, down a step, down a step, down a step. And when you get dressed, you put on first your stockings, then your shoes.

JULIETTE: Down at heel!

KING: And a dress. It's amazing . . .

JULIETTE: A cheap one. A tatty old thing!

KING: You don't know what you're saying! It's beautiful, a tatty old dress!

JULIETTE: Once I had an abscess in the mouth and they pulled out one of my teeth.

KING: You're in terrible pain. But it starts to ease off, and then disappears. It's a tremendous relief, it makes you feel wonderfully happy.

JULIETTE: I feel tired, tired, tired!

KING: So you take a rest. That's good.

JULIETTE: Not enough time off for that!

KING: You can still hope you'll have some, one day. . . . You go out with a basket and do the shopping. You say good day to the grocer.

JULIETTE: He's enormous! Hideously fat! So ugly he frightens the birds and the cats away.

KING: Marvelous! You take out your purse, you pay, and get your change. The market's a medley of green lettuce, red cherries, golden grapes and purple eggplants . . . all the colors of the rainbow! . . . It's extraordinary! Incredible! Like a fairy tale!

JULIETTE: And then I go home . . . the same way I came.

KING: You take the same road twice a day! With the sky above you! You can gaze at it twice a day. And you breathe the air. You never realize you're breathing. You must think about it. Remember! I'm sure it never crosses your mind. It's a miracle!

JULIETTE: And then, then I do the washing up from the day before. Plates smothered in sticky fat! And then I have the cooking to do.

KING: Sublime! *Inspiring awe*

JULIETTE: You're wrong. It's a bore. It makes me sick!

KING: It's a bore! Some people one can *never* understand! It's wonderful to feel bored and *not* to feel bored, too, to lose one's temper, and *not* to lose one's temper, to be *dis*contented and to be content. To practice resignation and to insist on your rights. You get excited, you talk and people talk to you, you touch and they touch you. All this is magical, like some endless celebration.

JULIETTE: You're right there. There's no end to it! After that, I still have to wait at table.

KING (*still rapturously*): You wait at table! You wait at table! What do you serve at table?

JULIETTE: The meal I've just prepared.

KING: What, for example?

JULIETTE: I don't know, the main dish. Stew!

KING: Stew! Stew! (*Dreamily.*)

JULIETTE: It's a meal in itself.

KING: I used to be so fond of stew, with vegetables and potatoes, cabbage and carrots all mixed up with butter, crushed with a fork and mashed together.

JULIETTE: We could bring him some.

KING: Send for some stew!

MARGUERITE: No.

JULIETTE: But if he likes it.

DOCTOR: Bad for his health. He's on a diet.

KING: I want some stew.

DOCTOR: It's not what the doctor orders for a dying man.

MARIE: But if it's his last wish . . .

MARGUERITE: He must detach himself.

KING: Gravy . . . hot potatoes . . . and carrots to lead me by the nose . . .

JULIETTE: He's still making jokes.

KING (*wearily*): Till now, I'd never noticed how beautiful carrots were. (*To* JULIETTE:) Quick! Go and kill the two spiders in my bedroom! I don't want them to survive me. No, don't kill them! Perhaps in *them* there's something still of *me* . . . it's dead, that stew . . . vanished from the universe. There never was such a thing as stew.

GUARD (*announcing*): Stew has been banished from the length and breadth of the land.

MARGUERITE: At last, something achieved! At least he's given *that* up! Of all the things we crave for, the minor ones go first. Now we can begin. Gently, as you remove a dressing from an open sore, first lifting the corners, because they're furthest from the center of the wound. (*Approaching the* KING.) Juliette, wipe the sweat from his face, he's dripping wet. (*To* MARIE:) No, not you!

DOCTOR (*to* MARGUERITE): It's panic oozing through his pores.

He examines the sick man, while MARIE *might kneel for a moment, covering her face with her hands.*

You see, his temperature's gone down, though there's not much sign of goose flesh. His hair was standing on end before. Now it's resting and lying flat. He's not used to being so terrified yet, oh no! But now he can see the fear inside him; that's why he's dared to close his eyes. He'll open them again. He still looks tense, but see how the wrinkles of old age are settling on his face. Already he's letting things take their course. He'll still have a few setbacks. It's not as quick as all that. But he won't have the wind up any more. That would have been too degrading. He'll still be subject to fright, but pure fright, without abdominal complications. We can't hope this death will be an example to others. But it will be fairly respectable. His *death* will kill him now, and not his fear. We'll have to help him all the same, your Majesty, he'll need a lot of help, till the very last second, till he's drawn his very last breath.

MARGUERITE: I'll help him. I'll drive it out of him. I'll cut him loose. I'll untie every knot and ravel out the tangled skein. I'll separate the wheat from the tenacious tares that cling to him and bind him.

[DOCTOR: It won't be easy.

MARGUERITE: Where on earth did he pick up all these weeds, these trailing creepers?

DOCTOR: They've grown up slowly, through the years.

MARGUERITE: You've settled down nicely now, your Majesty. Don't you feel more peaceful?

MARIE (*standing up, to the* KING): Until Death comes, you are still *here*. When Death is here, *you* will have gone. You won't meet her or see her.

MARGUERITE: The lies of life, those old fallacies! We've heard them all before. Death has always been here, present in the seed since the very first day. She is the

shoot that grows, the flower that blows, the only fruit we know.

MARIE (*to* MARGUERITE): That's a basic truth too, and we've heard *that* before!

MARGUERITE: It's a basic truth. And the ultimate truth, isn't it, Doctor?

DOCTOR: What you both say is true. It depends on the point of view.

MARIE (*to the* KING): You used to believe me, once.

KING: I'm dying.

DOCTOR: He's changed *his* point of view. He's shifted his position.

MARIE: If you've to look at it from both sides, look at it from my side too.

KING: I'm dying. I can't. I'm dying.

MARIE: Oh! My power over him is going.]

MARGUERITE (*to* MARIE): Neither your charm nor your charms can bewitch the King any more.

GUARD (*announcing*): The Charm of Queen Marie no longer casts its spell over the King.

MARIE (*to the* KING): You used to love me, you love me still, as I have always loved you.

MARGUERITE: She thinks of no one but herself.

JULIETTE: That's human nature.

MARIE: I've always loved you, I love you still.

KING: I don't know why, but that doesn't seem to help.

DOCTOR: Love is mad.

Explain characters and what the mean in real life

MARIE (*to the* KING): Love *is* mad. And if you're mad with love, if you love blindly, completely, death will steal away. If you love me, if you love everything, love will consume your fear. Love lifts you up, you let yourself go and fear lets go of you. The whole universe is one, everything lives again and the cup that was drained is full.

KING: I'm full all right, but full of holes. I'm a honeycomb of cavities that are widening, deepening into bottomless pits. It makes me dizzy to look down the gaping gulfs inside me. I'm coming to an end.

MARIE: There is no end. Others will take your place and gaze at the sky for *you*.

KING: I'm dying.

MARIE: Become these other beings, and live in them. There's always something here . . . something . . .

KING: What's that?

MARIE: Something that exists. *That* never perishes.

KING: And yet there's still . . . there's still . . . there's still so little left.

MARIE: The younger generation's expanding the universe.

KING: I'm dying.

MARIE: Conquering new constellations.

KING: I'm dying.

MARIE: Boldly battering at the gates of Heaven.

KING: They can knock them flat for all I care!

DOCTOR: They've also started making elixirs of immortality.

KING (*to the* DOCTOR): Incompetent fool! Why didn't *you* discover them before?

MARIE: New suns are about to appear.

KING: It makes me wild!

MARIE: Brand-new stars. Virgin stars.

KING: They'll fade away. Anyhow, I don't care!

GUARD (announcing): Constellations old or new no longer interest His Majesty, King Berenger!

MARIE: A new science is coming into being.

KING: *I'm* dying.

[MARIE: A new wisdom's taking the place of the old, a stupidity and ignorance greater than before, different of course but still the same. Let that console you and rejoice your heart.

KING: I'm frightened, I'm dying.

MARIE: You laid the foundations for all this.

KING: I didn't do it on purpose.]

MARIE: You were a pioneer, a guide, a harbinger of all these new developments. You count. And you will be counted.

KING: I'll never be the accountant. I'm dying.

MARIE: Everything that has been will be, everything that will be is, everything that will be has been. You are inscribed forever in the annals of the universe.

KING: Who'll look up those old archives? I die, so let everything die! No, let everything stay as it is! No, let everything die, if my death won't resound through worlds without end! Let everything die! No, let everything remain!

GUARD: His Majesty the King wants the remains to remain.

KING: No, let it all die!

GUARD: His Majesty the King wants it all to die!

KING: Let it all die with me! No, let it all survive me! No, let it all stay, let it all die, stay, die!

MARGUERITE: He doesn't know *what* he wants.

JULIETTE: I don't think he knows what he wants *any more*.

DOCTOR: He no longer *knows* what he wants. His brain's degenerating, he's senile, gaga.

GUARD (*announcing*): His Majesty has gone ga . . .

MARGUERITE (*to the* GUARD, *interrupting him*): Idiot, be quiet! We want no more doctors' bulletins given to the press. [People would only laugh, those who are still here to laugh and to listen. The rest of the world can pick up your words by radio, and they're quite jubilant.]

GUARD (*announcing*): Doctors' bulletins suspended by order of Her Majesty Queen Marguerite.

MARIE (*to the* KING): My King, my little King. . . .

KING: When I had nightmares and cried in my sleep, you would wake me up, kiss me and smooth away my fears.

MARGUERITE: She can't do that now!

KING: When I had sleepless nights and wandered out of my room, you would wake up too. In your pink-flowered dressing gown, you'd come and find me in the throne room, take me by the hand and lead me back to bed.

JULIETTE: It was just the same with my husband.

KING: I used to share my colds with you and the flu.

MARGUERITE: You won't catch colds now!

KING: In the morning we used to open our eyes at the very same moment. I shall close them alone, or not have *you* beside me. We used to think the same things at the same time. And you'd finish a sentence I'd just started in my head. I'd call you to rub my back when I was in the bath. And you'd choose my ties for me. Though I didn't always like them. We used to fight about that. No one knew, and no one ever will.

[DOCTOR: A storm in a teacup.

MARGUERITE: How suburban! We'll have to draw a veil over *that*!

KING (*to* MARIE): You'd hate my hair to be untidy. You used to comb it for me.

JULIETTE: It's so romantic, all this.

MARGUERITE: You hair won't be untidy now!

JULIETTE: But it's really very sad.

KING: Then you'd dust my crown and polish the pearls to make them shine.]

MARIE (*to the* KING): Do you love me? Do you love me? I've always loved *you*. Do you still love *me*? He *does* still love me. Do you love me today? Do you love me this minute? Here I am. . . . Here. . . . I'm here. . . .

Look! Look! . . . Take a good look! . . . Well, *look* at me!

KING: I've always loved myself, at least I can still love myself, feel myself, see myself, contemplate myself.

[MARGUERITE (*to* MARIE): That's enough! (*To the* KING:) You must stop looking back. That's a piece of advice. Or hurry and get it over. Soon this will be an order. (*To* MARIE:) I've told you before. From now on you can't do him anything but harm.]

DOCTOR (*looking at his watch*): He's running late . . . he's turned back in his tracks.

MARGUERITE: It's not serious. Don't worry, Doctor, Executioner. His little tricks, these kicks against the pricks . . . it was all to be expected, all part of the program.

DOCTOR: If this was a good old heart attack, we wouldn't have had so much trouble.

MARGUERITE: Heart attacks are reserved for businessmen.

DOCTOR: . . . or even double pneumonia!

MARGUERITE: That's for the poor, not for kings.

KING: I could decide not to die.

JULIETTE: You see, he's not cured yet.

KING: What if I decided to stop wanting things, to just stop wanting, and decided not to decide!

[MARGUERITE: We could decide for you.

GUARD (*announcing*): The Queen and the Doctor no longer owe the King obedience.

DOCTOR: We owe him *dis*obedience.

KING: Who except the King can release you from your duty to the King?

MARGUERITE: Force can do that, the force of events. First principles dictate their own commandments.

DOCTOR (*to* MARGUERITE): First principles and commandments are now invested in us.]

GUARD (*while* JULIETTE *starts pushing the* KING *around the stage in his invalid chair*): It was His Majesty, my Commander in Chief, who set the Thames on fire. It was he who invented gunpowder and stole fire from the gods. He nearly blew the whole place up. But he caught the pieces and tied them together again with string. I helped him, but it wasn't so easy. *He* wasn't so easy either. He was the one who fitted up the first forges on earth. He discovered the way to make steel. He used to work eighteen hours a day. And he made *us* work even harder. He was our chief engineer. As an engineer he made the first balloon, and then the zeppelin. And finally, with his own hands, he built the first airplane. At the start it wasn't a success. The first test pilots, Icarus and the rest, all fell into the sea. Till eventually he piloted the plane himself. I was his mechanic. Long before that, when he was only a little prince, he'd invented the wheelbarrow. I used to play with him. Then rails and railways and automobiles. He drew up the plans for the Eiffel Tower, not to mention his designs for the sickle and the plough, the harvesters and the tractors.

KING: Tractors? Good Heavens, yes! I'd forgotten.

GUARD: He extinguished volcanoes and caused new ones to erupt. He built Rome, New York, Moscow and Geneva. He *founded* Paris. He created revolutions, counter-revolutions, religion, reform and counter-reform.

JULIETTE: You wouldn't think so to look at him.

KING: What's an automobile?

JULIETTE (*still pushing him in his wheel chair*): It runs along by itself.

GUARD: He wrote tragedies and comedies, under the name of Shakespeare.

JULIETTE: Oh, so that's who Shakespeare was!

DOCTOR (*to the* GUARD): You ought to have told us before! Think how long we've been racking our brains to find out!

GUARD: It was a secret. He wouldn't let me. He invented the telephone and the telegraph, and fixed them up himself. He did everything with his own hands.

JULIETTE: He was never any good with his hands! He used to call the plumber at the slightest sign of a leak!

GUARD: My Commander in Chief was a very handy man!

JULIETTE: Now he can't even get his shoes on. Or off!

GUARD: Not so long ago he managed to split the atom.

JULIETTE: Now he can't even turn the light off. Or on!

GUARD: Majesty, Commander in Chief, Master, Managing Director . . .

MARGUERITE (*to the* GUARD): We know all about his earlier exploits. We don't need an inventory.

The GUARD *returns to his post.*

KING (*while he is being pushed around*): What's a horse?

. . . Those are windows, those are walls and this is the floor. I've done such things! What do they say I did? I don't remember what I did. I forget, I forget. (*While he is still being pushed around*:) And that's a throne.

MARIE: Do you remember me? I'm here, I'm here.

KING: I'm here. I exist.

JULIETTE: He doesn't even remember what a horse is.

KING: I remember a little ginger cat.

MARIE: He remembers a cat.

KING: I used to have a little ginger cat. We called him our wandering Jew. I had found him in a field, stolen from his mother, a real wildcat. He was two weeks old, or a little more, but he knew how to scratch and bite. He was quite fierce. I fed him and stroked him and took him home and he grew into the gentlest of cats. Once, Madame, he crept into the coat sleeve of a lady visitor. He was the politest of creatures, a natural politeness, like a prince. When we came home in the middle of the night he used to come and greet us with his eyes full of sleep. Then he'd stumble off back to his box. In the morning he'd wake us up to crawl into our bed. [One day we'd shut the bedroom door. He tried so hard to open it, shoving his little behind against it. He got so angry and made a terrible row; he sulked for a week.] He was scared stiff of the vacuum cleaner. A bit of a coward really, that cat; defenseless, a poet cat. We bought him a clockwork mouse. He started by sniffing it anxiously. When we wound it up and the mouse began to move, he spat at it, then took to his heels and crouched under the wardrobe. [When he'd grown up, his lady friends would pace round the

house, courting and calling him. It used to frighten
him silly and he wouldn't move.] We tried to introduce
him to the outside world. We put him down on the
pavement near the window. He was terrified, afraid
of the pigeons that hopped all around him. There he
was, pressed against the wall, miaowing and crying to
me in desperation. To him, other animals and cats
were strange creatures he mistrusted or enemies he
feared. He only felt at home with us. [We were his
family. He was not afraid of men. He'd jump on their
shoulders without warning, and lick their hair.] He
thought *we* were cats and cats were something else.
And yet one fine day he must have felt the urge to go
out on his own. The neighbor's big dog killed him.
And there he was, like a toy cat, a twitching marionette with one eye gone and a paw torn off, yes, like
a doll destroyed by a sadistic child.

[MARIE (*to* MARGUERITE): You shouldn't have left the door
open; 1 warned you.

MARGUERITE: I hated that sentimental, timorous beast.

KING: How I missed him! He was good and beautiful and
wise, all the virtues. He loved me, he loved me. My
poor little cat, my one and only cat.]

*The lines about the cat should be spoken with as little
emotion as possible: to say them, the* KING *should
rather give an impression of being dazed, in a kind
of dreamy stupor, except perhaps in this very last
speech, which expresses a certain sorrow.*

[DOCTOR: I tell you he's running late.

MARGUERITE: I'm watching it. The timetable allows for
holdups. Some delays were expected, you know.]

KING: I used to dream about him . . . that he was lying in the grate, on the glowing embers, and Marie was surprised he didn't burn. I told her, "Cats don't burn, they're fireproof." He came miaowing out of the fireplace in a cloud of thick smoke. But it wasn't him any more. What a transformation! It was a different cat, fat and ugly. An enormous she-cat. Like his mother, the wildcat. A bit like Marguerite.

For a few moments JULIETTE *leaves the* KING *in his wheelchair downstage in the center, facing the audience.*

JULIETTE: It's a great pity, I must say, a real shame! He was such a good king.

DOCTOR: Far from easy to please. Really quite wicked. Revengeful and cruel.

MARGUERITE: Vain.

JULIETTE: There have been worse.

MARIE: He was gentle, he was tender.

GUARD: We were rather fond of him.

DOCTOR (*to the* GUARD *and to* JULIETTE): You both complained about him, though.

JULIETTE: That's forgotten now.

[DOCTOR: Several times I had to intervene on your behalf.

MARGUERITE: He only listened to Queen Marie.

DOCTOR: He was hard and severe, and not even just.

JULIETTE: We saw him so little. And yet we *did* see him, we saw him quite often really.

GUARD: He was strong. It's true he cut a few heads off.

JULIETTE: Not many.

GUARD: All for the public good.

DOCTOR: And the result? We're surrounded by enemies.

MARGUERITE: You can hear us crumbling away. We've lost our frontiers already, only an ever widening gulf cuts us off from our neighbors.

JULIETTE: It's better that way. Now they can't invade us.

MARGUERITE: We're poised over a gaping chasm. Nothing but a growing void all around us.

GUARD: We're still clinging to the earth's crust.

MARGUERITE: Not for long!

MARIE: Better to perish with him!

MARGUERITE: There's nothing but the crust left. We'll soon be adrift in space.]

DOCTOR: And it's all his fault! He never cared what came after him. He never thought about his successors. After him the deluge. Worse than the deluge, after him there's nothing! Selfish bungler!

JULIETTE: *De mortuis nihil nisi bene.* He was king of a great kingdom.

MARIE: He was the heart and center of it.

JULIETTE: Its royal residence.

GUARD: A kingdom that stretched for thousands of miles around. You couldn't even glimpse its boundaries.

JULIETTE: Boundless in space.

MARGUERITE: But bounded in time. At once infinite and ephemeral.

JULIETTE: He was its Prince, its First Gentleman, he was its father and its son. He was crowned King at the very moment of his birth.

MARIE: He and his kingdom grew up together.

MARGUERITE: And vanish together.

[JULIETTE: He was the King, master of all the universe.

DOCTOR: An unwise master, who didn't know his own kingdom.

MARGUERITE: He knew very little of it.

MARIE: It was too extensive.

JULIETTE: The earth collapses with him. The suns are growing dim. Water, fire, air, ours and every universe, the whole lot disappears. In what warehouse or cellar, junkroom or attic will there ever be room to store all this? It'll take up space all right!]

DOCTOR: When kings die, they clutch at the walls, the trees, the fountains, the moon. They pull themselves up. . . .

MARGUERITE: But it all crashes down.

GUARD: And disintegrates.

DOCTOR: It melts and evaporates, till there's not a drop left, not a speck of dust, not the faintest shadow.

[JULIETTE: He drags it all with him into the abyss.

MARIE: He'd organized his world so well. He hadn't quite become master of it. But he would have been. He's dying too soon. He'd divided the year into four seasons. He was really getting on very nicely. He'd thought up the trees and the flowers, all the perfumes and colors.

GUARD: A world fit for a king.

MARIE: He'd invented the oceans and the mountains: nearly sixteen thousand feet for Mont Blanc.

GUARD: Over twenty-nine thousand for the Himalayas.

MARIE: The leaves fell from the trees, but they grew again.

JULIETTE: That was clever.]

MARIE: The very day he was born, he created the sun.

JULIETTE: And that wasn't enough. He had to have fire made too.

MARGUERITE: And there were wide-open spaces, and there were stars, and the sky and oceans and mountains; and there were plains, there were cities, and people and faces and buildings and rooms and beds; and the light and the night; and there were wars and there was peace.

GUARD: And a throne.

MARIE: And his fingers.

MARGUERITE: The way he looked and the way he breathed.

JULIETTE: He's still breathing now.

MARIE: He's still breathing, because I'm here.

MARGUERITE (*to the* DOCTOR): Is he still breathing?

JULIETTE: Yes, your Majesty. He's still breathing, because we're here.

DOCTOR (*examining the invalid*): Yes, yes, no doubt about it. He's still breathing. His kidneys have stopped functioning, but the blood's still circulating. Going round and round. His heart is sound.

MARGUERITE: It'll have to stop soon. What's the good of a heart that has no reason to beat?

DOCTOR: You're right. His heart's gone berserk. D'you hear?

You can hear the frantic beatings of the King's heart.

There it is, racing away, then it slows down, then it's off again, as fast as it can go.

The beatings of the King's heart shake the house. The crack in the wall widens and others appear. A stretch of wall could collapse or vanish from sight.

JULIETTE: Good God! Everything's falling to pieces!

MARGUERITE: A mad heart, a madman's heart!

DOCTOR: A heart in a panic. It's infectious. Anyone can catch it.

MARGUERITE (*to* JULIETTE): It'll all be quiet in a moment.

DOCTOR: We know every phase of the disease. It's always like this when a universe snuffs out.

MARGUERITE (*to* MARIE): It proves his universe is not unique.

JULIETTE: That never entered his head.

MARIE: He's forgetting me. At this very moment he's forgetting me. I can feel it, he's leaving me behind. I'm nothing if he forgets me. I can't go on living if I don't exist in his distracted heart. Hold tight, hold firm! Clench your fists with all your strength! Don't let go of me!

JULIETTE: Now his strength has left him.

MARIE: Cling to me, don't let go! It's I who keep you alive. I keep *you* alive, you keep *me* alive. D'you see, d'you understand? If you forget me, if you abandon me, I no longer exist, I am nothing.

DOCTOR: He will be a page in a book of ten thousand pages in one of a million libraries which has a million books.

JULIETTE: It won't be easy to find that page again.

[DOCTOR: Oh yes, you'll find it catalogued by subject matter, in alphabetical order . . . until the day comes when the paper's turned to dust . . . unless it's destroyed by fire. Libraries often go up in smoke.]

JULIETTE: He's clenching his fists. He's hanging on. He's still resisting. He's coming back to consciousness.

MARIE: He's not coming back to me.

JULIETTE (*to* MARIE): Your voice is waking him up, his eyes are open. He's looking at you.

DOCTOR: Yes, his heart's ticking over again.

[MARGUERITE: He's in a fine state! A dying man trapped in a thicket of thorns. A thicket of thorns! How can we pull him out? (*To the* KING:) You're stuck in the mud, caught in the brambles.

JULIETTE: And when he does get free, he'll leave his shoes behind.]

MARIE: Hold me tight, as I hold you! Look at me, as I look at you!

The KING *looks at her.*

MARGUERITE: She's getting you all mixed up. Forget about her and you'll feel better.

DOCTOR: Give in, your Majesty. Abdicate, Majesty.

JULIETTE: You'd better abdicate, if you must.

JULIETTE *pushes him round in his chair again and stops in front of* MARIE.

KING: I can hear, I can see, who are you? Are you my mother? My sister? My wife? My daughter? My niece? My cousin? . . . I know *you* . . . I'm sure I *do* know you.

They turn him to face MARGUERITE.

You hateful, hideous woman! Why are you still with me? Why are you leaning over me? Go away, go away!

MARIE: Don't look at her! Turn your eyes on me, and keep them wide open! Hope! I'm here. Remember who you are! I'm Marie.

KING (*to* MARIE): Marie!?

MARIE: If you don't remember, gaze at me and learn again that I am Marie. Look at my eyes, my face, my hair, my arms! And learn me off by heart!

MARGUERITE: You're upsetting him. He's past learning anything now.

MARIE (*to the* KING): If I can't hold you back, at least turn and look at me! I'm here! Keep this picture of me in your mind and take it with you!

MARGUERITE: He could never drag that around, he hasn't got the strength. It's too heavy for a ghost, [and we can't let other ghosts oppress him. He'd collapse under the weight. His ghost would bleed to death. He wouldn't be able to move.] He's got to travel light. (*To the* KING:) Throw everything away, lighten the load.

DOCTOR: [It's time he began to get rid of the ballast.] Lighten the load, your Majesty.

The KING *rises to his feet, but he has a different way of moving, his gestures are jerky, he already begins to look rather like a sleepwalker. The movements of a sleepwalker will become more and more pronounced.*

KING: Marie?

MARGUERITE (*to* MARIE): You see, your name means nothing to him now.

GUARD: Marie's name now means nothing to the King.

KING: Marie! (*As he pronounces this name, he can stretch out his arms and then let them fall again.*)

MARIE: He's said it.

DOCTOR: Repeated it, but without understanding.

JULIETTE: Like a parrot. Sounds that are dead.

KING (*to* MARGUERITE, *turning toward her*): I don't know you, I don't love you.

JULIETTE: He knows what not knowing means.

MARGUERITE (*to* MARIE): He'll start his journey with a picture of *me* in his mind. That won't get in his way. [It will leave him when it has to.] It's fitted with a gadget that's worked by remote control. (*To the* KING:) Have another look!

The KING *turns toward the audience.*

MARIE: He can't see you.

MARGUERITE: He won't see *you* any more.

By some theatrical trick, MARIE *suddenly disappears.*

JULIETTE: He can't see any more.

DOCTOR (*examining the* KING): That's true, he's lost his sight.

. *He has been moving his finger in front of the King's eyes; or perhaps a lighted candle or a match or a cigarette lighter held in front of Berenger's eyes. They stare out vacantly.*

JULIETTE: He can't see any more. The Doctor has made an official pronouncement.

GUARD: His Majesty is officially blind.

[MARGUERITE: He'll see better if he looks inside himself.

KING: I can see things and faces and towns and forests, I can see space, I can see time.

MARGUERITE: Look a little further.

KING: I can't see any further.

JULIETTE: His horizon's closing in, blocking his view.

MARGUERITE: Cast your eyes beyond what you can see. Behind the road, through the mountain, away beyond that forest, the one you never cleared for cultivation.

KING: The ocean, I daren't go any further, I can't swim.

DOCTOR: Not enough exercise!

MARGUERITE: That's only the surface of things. Look deep inside them.]

KING: There's a mirror in my entrails where everything's reflected, I can see more and more, I can see the world, I can see life slipping away.

MARGUERITE: Look beyond the reflection.

KING: I see myself. Behind everything, I exist. Nothing

but me everywhere. [I am the earth, I am the sky, I am
the wind, I am the fire;] am I in every mirror or am
I the mirror of everything?

JULIETTE: He loves himself too much.

DOCTOR: A well-known disease of the psyche: narcissism.

[MARGUERITE: Come nearer.

KING: There isn't a path.

JULIETTE: He can hear. He's turning his head as he speaks,
he's trying to listen, he's stretching out an arm, and
now the other.]

GUARD: What's he trying to take hold of?

JULIETTE: He wants something to lean on.

For a few moments the KING *has been advancing like
a blind man, with very unsteady steps.*

KING: Where are the walls? Where are the arms? Where
are the doors? Where are the windows?

JULIETTE: The walls are here, your Majesty, we are all here.
Here's an arm for you.

JULIETTE *leads the* KING *to the left, and helps him
touch the wall.*

KING: The wall is here. The scepter!

JULIETTE *gives it to him.*

JULIETTE: Here it is!

KING: Guard, where are you? Answer me!

GUARD: Still yours to command, your Majesty. Yours to
command.

The KING *takes a few steps toward the* GUARD. *He touches him.*

Yes, yes, I'm here. Yes, yes, I'm here.

JULIETTE: Your apartments are this way, your Majesty.

GUARD: I swear we'll never leave you, Majesty.

The GUARD *suddenly disappears.*

JULIETTE: We're here beside you, we'll stay with you.

JULIETTE *suddenly disappears.*

KING: Guard! Juliette! Answer me! I can't hear you any more. Doctor, Doctor, am I going deaf?

DOCTOR: No, your Majesty, not yet.

KING: Doctor!

DOCTOR: Forgive me, your Majesty, I must go. I'm afraid I have to. I'm very sorry, please forgive me.

The DOCTOR *retires. He goes out bowing, like a marionette, through the upstage door on the right. He has gone out backward, with much bowing and scraping, still excusing himself.*

KING: His voice is getting faint and the sound of his footsteps is fading, he's gone!

MARGUERITE: He's a doctor, with professional obligations.

Before she left, JULIETTE *must have pushed the wheel chair into a corner so it is not in the way.*

KING (*stretching out his arms*): Where are the others? (*The* KING *reaches the downstage door on the right, then makes for the downstage door on the left.*) They've gone and they've shut me in.

MARGUERITE: They were a nuisance, all those people. They were in your way, hanging around you, getting under your feet. Admit they got on your nerves!

The KING *is walking rather more easily.*

KING: I need their services.

MARGUERITE: I'll take their place. I'm the queen of all trades.

KING: I didn't give anyone leave to go. Make them come back, call them.

[MARGUERITE: They've been cut off. It's what you wanted.

KING: It's not what I wanted.]

MARGUERITE: They could never have gone away if you hadn't wanted them to. You can't go back on your decision now. You've dropped them.

KING: Let them come back!

MARGUERITE: You've even forgotten their names. What were they called?

The KING *is silent.*

How many were there?

KING: Who do you mean? . . . I don't like being shut in. Open the doors.

MARGUERITE: A little patience. The doors will soon be open wide.

KING (*after a silence*): The doors . . . the doors . . . what doors?

MARGUERITE: Were there once some doors? Was there once a world, were you ever alive?

KING: I am.

MARGUERITE: Keep still. Moving tires you.

The KING *does as she says.*

KING: I am. . . . Sounds, echoes, coming from a great distance, fainter and fainter, dying away. I am deaf.

MARGUERITE: You can still hear *me,* you'll hear me all the better.

The KING *is standing motionless, without a word.*

Sometimes you have a dream. And you get involved, you believe in it, you love it. In the morning, when you open your eyes, the two worlds are still confused. The brilliance of the light blurs the faces of the night. You'd like to remember, you'd like to hold them back. But they slip between your fingers, the brutal reality of day drives them away. What did I dream about, you ask yourself? What was it happened? Who was I kissing? Who did I love? What was I saying and what was I told? Then you find you're left with a vague regret for all those things that were or seemed to have been. You no longer know what it was that was there all around you. You no longer know.

KING: I no longer know what was there all around me. I know I was part of a world, and this world was all about me. I know it was me and what else was there, what else?

MARGUERITE: There are still some cords that bind you which I haven't yet untied. Or which I haven't cut. There are still some hands that cling to you and hold you back. (*Moving around the* KING, MARGUERITE *cuts the space, as though she had a pair of invisible scissors in her hand.*)

KING: Me. Me. Me.

MARGUERITE: This you is not the real you. It's an odd collection of bits and pieces, horrid things that live on you like parasites. The mistletoe that grows on the bough is not the bough, the ivy that climbs the wall is not the wall. You're sagging under the load, your shoulders are bent, that's what makes you feel so old. And it's that ball and chain dragging at your feet which make it so difficult to walk. (MARGUERITE *leans down and removes an invisible ball and chain from the King's feet, then as she gets up she looks as though she were making a great effort to lift the weight.*) A ton weight, they must weigh at least a ton. (*She pretends to be throwing them in the direction of the audience; then, freed of the weight, she straightens up.*) That's better! How did you manage to trail them around all your life?

The KING *tries to straighten up.*

And I used to wonder why you were so round-shouldered! It's because of that sack! (MARGUERITE *pretends to be taking a sack from the King's shoulders and throws it away.*) And that heavy pack. (MARGUERITE *goes through the same motions for the pack.*) And that spare pair of army boots.

KING (*with a sort of grunt*): No.

MARGUERITE: Don't get so excited! You won't need an extra pair of boots any more. Or that rifle, or that machine gun. (*The same procedure as for the pack.*) Or that tool box. (*Same procedure: protestations from the* KING.) He seems quite attached to it! A nasty rusty old saber. (*She takes it off him, although the* KING *tries grumpily to stop her.*) Leave it all to me and be a good boy. (*She taps on the King's hand.*) You don't need self-defense any more. No one wants to hurt you now. All those thorns and splinters in your cloak, those creepers and seaweed and slimy wet leaves. How they stick to you! I'll pick them off, I'll pull them away. What dirty marks they make! (*She goes through the motions of picking and pulling them off.*) The dreamer comes out of his dream. There you are! Now I've got rid of all those messy little things that worried you. Now your cloak's more beautiful, we've cleaned you up. You look much better for it. Now have a little walk. Give me your hand, give me your hand then! Don't be afraid any more, let yourself go! I'll see you don't fall. You don't dare!

KING (*in a kind of stammer*): Me.

MARGUERITE: Oh no! He imagines he's *everything!* He thinks *his* existence is *all* existence. I'll have to drive *that* out of his head! (*Then, as if to encourage him:*) Nothing will be forgotten. It's all quite safe in a mind that needs no memories. A grain of salt that dissolves in water doesn't disappear: it makes the water salty. Ah, that's it! Straighten up! Now you're not round-shouldered, no more pains in your back, no more stiffness! Wasn't it a heavy weight to bear? Now you feel better. You can go forward now, go on! Come along, give me your hand!

The King's shoulders are slowly rounding again.

Don't hunch your shoulders, you've no more loads to bear. . . . Oh, those conditioned reflexes, so hard to shake off! . . . You've no more weight on your shoulders, I tell you. Stand up straight! (*She helps him to straighten up.*) Your hand! . . .

The KING *is undecided.*

How disobedient he is! Don't clench your fists like
that! Open your fingers out! What are you holding?
(*She unclenches his fingers.*) He's holding the whole
kingdom in his hand. In miniature: on microfilm . . .
in tiny grains. (*To the* KING:) That grain won't grow
again, it's bad seed! They're all moldy! Drop them!
Unclasp your fingers! I order you to loosen those
fingers! Let go of the plains, let go of the mountains!
Like this. They were only dust. (*She takes him by the
hand and drags him away, in spite of some slight
resistance still from the* KING.) Come along! Still trying to resist! Where does he find all this will power?
No, don't try to lie down! Don't sit down either! No
reason why you should stumble. I'll guide you, don't
be frightened! (*She guides him across the stage, holding him by the hand.*) You can do it now, can't you?
It's easy, isn't it? I've had a gentle slope made for you.
It gets steeper later on, but that doesn't matter. You'll
have your strength back by then. Don't turn your head
to see what you'll never see again, think hard, con-
centrate on your heart, keep right on, you must!

KING (*advancing with his eyes closed, still held by the
hand*): The Empire . . . has there ever been another
Empire like it? With two suns, two moons and two
heavens to light it. And there's another sun rising,
and there's another! A third firmament appearing,
shooting up and fanning out! As one sun sets, others
are rising . . . dawn and twilight all at once. . . .
Beyond the seven hundred and seventy-seven poles.

MARGUERITE: Go further, further, further. Toddle on,
toddle on, go on!

KING: Blue, blue.

MARGUERITE: He can still distinguish colors. (*To the* KING:)
Give up this Empire too! And give your colors up!
They're leading you astray, holding you back. You
can't linger any longer, you can't stop again, you
mustn't! (*She moves away from the* KING.) Walk by
yourself! Don't be frightened! Go on! (MARGUERITE,
from one corner of the stage, is directing the KING *at
a distance.*) It's not the day now or the night, there's
no more day and no more night. Try and follow that
wheel that's spinning around in front of you! Don't
lose sight of it, follow it! But not too close, it's all in
flames, you might get burnt. Go forward! I'll move
the undergrowth aside. Watch out! Don't bump into
that phantom on your right . . . clutching hands, im-
ploring hands, pitiful arms and hands, don't you come
back, away with you! Don't touch him, or I'll strike
you! (*To the* KING:) Don't turn your head! Skirt the
precipice on your left, and don't be afraid of that
howling wolf . . . his fangs are made of cardboard,
he doesn't exist. (*To the wolf:*) Wolf, cease to exist!
(*To the* KING:) Don't be afraid of the rats now either!
They can't bite your toes. (*To the rats:*) Rats and
vipers, cease to exist! (*To the* KING:) And don't start
pitying that beggar who's holding out his hand! . . .
Beware of that old woman coming toward you! . . .
Don't take that glass of water she's offering! You're
not thirsty. (*To the imaginary old woman:*) He has no
need to quench his thirst, my good woman, he's not
thirsty. Don't stand in his way! Vanish! (*To the* KING:)
Climb over the fence . . . that big truck won't run
you over, it's a mirage . . . cross now. . . . Why no,
daisies don't sing, even in the spring. I'll smother
their cries. I'll obliterate them! . . . And stop listening

to the babbling of that brook! It's not real anyway, it's deceiving you . . . false voices, be still! (*To the* KING:) No one's calling you now. Smell that flower for the last time, then throw it away! Forget its perfume! Now you've lost the power of speech. Who's left for you to talk to? Yes, that's right. Put your best foot forward! Now the other! There's a footbridge. No, you won't feel giddy.

The KING *is advancing toward the steps of the throne.*

Hold yourself straight! You don't need your stick, besides you haven't got one. Don't bend down and whatever you do, don't fall! Up, up you go!

The KING *starts to climb the three or four steps to the throne.*

Higher, up again, up you go, still higher, higher, higher!

The KING *is quite close to the throne.*

Now turn and face me! Look at me! Look right through me! Gaze into my unreflecting mirror and stand up straight! . . . Give me your legs! The right one! Now the left!

As she gives him these orders, the KING *stiffens his legs.*

Give me a finger! Give me two fingers . . . three, four . . . five . . . all ten fingers! Now let me have your right arm! Your left arm! Your chest, your two shoulders and your stomach!

The KING *is motionless, still as a statue.*

There you are, you see! Now you've lost the power of speech, there's no need for your heart to beat, no

more need to breathe. It was a lot of fuss about nothing, wasn't it? Now you can take your place.

Sudden disappearance of QUEEN MARGUERITE *on the left. The* KING *is seated on his throne. During this final scene, the doors, windows and walls of the throne room will have slowly disappeared. This part of the action is very important.*

Now there is nothing on the stage except the KING *on his throne in a grayish light. Then the* KING *and his throne also disappear.*

Finally, there is nothing but the gray light.

This disappearance of the windows, the doors and the walls, the KING *and the throne must be very marked, but happen slowly and gradually. The* KING *sitting on his throne should remain visible for a short time before fading into a kind of mist.*